THE
Exceptional
Individual

THE
Exceptional
Individual

ACHIEVING
BUSINESS SUCCESS
ONE PERSON AT A TIME

PETER ENGEL

ST. MARTIN'S PRESS

NEW YORK

A THOMAS DUNNE BOOK.
An imprint of St. Martin's Press.

THE EXCEPTIONAL INDIVIDUAL: ACHIEVING BUSINESS SUCCESS ONE PERSON
AT A TIME. Copyright © 1998 by Peter Engel. All rights reserved.
Printed in the United States of America. No part of this book may be
used or reproduced in any manner whatsoever without written
permission except in the case of brief quotations embodied in critical
articles or reviews. For information, address St. Martin's Press,
175 Fifth Avenue, New York, N.Y. 10010.

Design by Ellen R. Sasahara

Library of Congress Cataloging-in-Publication Data

Engel, Peter H.
    The exceptional individual : achieving business success one person
at a time / Peter Engel.
        p.   cm.
    ISBN 0-312-18238-4
    1. Creative ability in business.   2. Achievement motivation.
    3. Success.   4. Entrepreneurship.   5. Executive ability.   I. Title.
    HD53.E54   1998
    650.1—dc21   97-37739
                                                                      CIP

First Edition: July 1998

10 9 8 7 6 5 4 3 2 1

To Brenda...*A LOT!*

CONTENTS

CONTENTS

THE
Exceptional
Individual

1

REAL EXCELLENCE

In 1982, Thomas Peters and Robert Waterman, successful members of the prestigious consulting firm of McKinsey & Company, wrote *In Search of Excellence*, in which they identified forty-three companies that typified excellence and a further nineteen that did not. The book became one of the all-time biggest sellers among business books. Peters left McKinsey and became an instant guru, a talk-show smash. He became *the* high-priced consultant called in by companies who were looking for easy answers to problems created by their own complacent failure to keep up with a changing world.

Executives searching for answers by reading *In Search of Excellence* found two insights of enormous value. The first was that Peters and Waterman boiled down the technique for achieving guaranteed business excellence into eight simple, nonthreatening "lessons." Moreover, these lessons felt good to readers because they were comfortable business clichés, such as "Stick to your knitting" and "Stay close to the customer." They were harmless enough in themselves and general enough to be unexceptionable.

In addition, Peters and Waterman went a lot farther than merely stating what made companies excellent. They

1

actually proved that their eight rules really worked by analyzing the "excellent" companies they chose—and showing that all of them achieved their excellence by sticking to those rules. The book was a tour de force. It was just complicated enough to challenge readers but easy enough to be understood by anyone who made a serious attempt. Of course the best part was that, when you did understand, why, there were the simple rules—tested and proven. If you followed them and they worked, great! And if not, well, who could blame you? After all, you had followed the most widely accepted guru of them all. No wonder Peters's eight clichés were adopted by any number of increasingly desperate American companies as something akin to the Ten Commandments.

Peters's eight "attributes of excellence" were all theoretically embodied by the forty-three solid pillars of corporate success the authors had selected. Without question it was a sort of self-fulfilling prophecy of corporate excellence. *In Search of Excellence* contained a paint-by-the-numbers mystique that, although a bit vague and open to interpretation, was easily packaged and sold to corporate America. If you were beginning to feel the hot breath of international competition and were getting the uneasy feeling that something might be terribly wrong with your approach, then it was more than comforting to hear Peters identify your problem as nothing more than structure gone awry. "American companies are being stymied," read the book, "by their structures and systems . . . which inhibit action." In fairness, Peters and Waterman also indicted the staffs of such "inhibited" companies, but only in the context of their structure, not because of their individual limitations. It would have been far too upsetting to the book's readers to be told that *they* might be at fault.

Throughout, there was the reassurance to every bureaucratic executive who read the book (or just the reviews, for that matter) that success in business springs from enlightened business tactics rather than from the individual effort of people who work within a particular company and make it grow. In other words, if things went wrong, it wasn't your fault.

The only trouble with Peters and Waterman's theories was that they proved to be dramatically wrong.

In 1984, *Business Week* magazine published an embarrassing cover story entitled "Oops!", which noted that many of Peters's "excellent" companies were no longer quite so excellent. Indeed, fourteen of forty-three were on the ropes only two years after being cited in his list. If excellence includes the ability of a business to stay healthy (and if it doesn't, then what on earth can it possibly mean?), then Peters's rules seemed poor descriptors indeed. His excellent companies—Delta Airlines, Texas Instruments, Atari, Digital Equipment Corporation, Eastman Kodak, and several others—were already very excellently hemorrhaging money.

But Peters's concepts were too seductive, and the army of consultants selling them (or selling their own, similarly simplistic "rules" about structure) were too persuasive. Corporate America would not listen to the view that *people*, not structure, create success. Thus, Peters continued to churn out a steady stream of book sequels, spin-offs, videotapes, and television and lecture appearances even as other "excellent" companies tumbled out of his list of forty-three. For several years, IBM became a classic example of wasted opportunity, wasted money, wasted people. Only after a completely new management team was appointed, and the company's ways of doing business drastically changed, was it rescued from the brink of destruction and revived. Wang Laboratories, having no such luck, went into bankruptcy. Atari—don't even ask. Oh, Tom!

Within a dozen years of the publication of *In Search of Excellence*, of the forty-three companies adjudged excellent, I judge that seventeen had fallen into significant difficulty, and a further seven have been, to be polite, lackluster. Of course, since then there have been other changes: "Bad" companies have fared well; "good" companies have done badly. Ironically, for the first twelve years after publication, Peters and Waterman's criteria for excellence proved to be a better predictor of failure and mediocrity than of success. Thereafter, their predictions are simply meaningless. Thus, I doubt that anyone would seriously question my proposition that *In Search of Excellence* was clearly and dangerously wrong. Peters's bundle of clichés was simple and trendy. But as an operating strategy, those rules and others like them contributed to more than a decade of wrongheaded thinking about excellence in business. The question that now needs answering is, What went wrong? and, in a broader context, What *does* cause a business to succeed—or fail?

MR. BUSINESS CONSULTANT, I KNEW YE WELL

Among the most popular myths (some would say frauds) of the 1980s and 1990s was the concept that some companies are much more successful than others because their bureaucracies, not their individuals, are progressive. Hundreds of American business consultants became rich hocking this idea to businesspeople the world over. And thousands of perfectly good firms got deeply into trouble thanks to this wrongheaded advice.

More new management consulting firms were formed in

the past fifteen years than at any other time in history. Business management consultants increased their revenues from $2.25 billion in 1980 to almost $16 billion in 1996, according to Kennedy Publications' directory of management consultants. And the growth continues unabated. This is astonishing when you consider the palpable lack of success most consulting proposals generate.

Some consultants, notably the incredibly successful Michael Hammer, author of the concept and book called *Reengineering the Corporation*, even warned clearly and loudly that their approach was *not* a system, but nevertheless that caveat was ignored. "Reengineering is centered on how work is done, not how an organization is structured," Hammer wrote in a later book, describing the revolution he started. "Reengineering is also not a fad, not merely the latest in a long line of short-lived management panaceas," he added hopefully. His warning was actually a repetition of the clear statement he and James Champy made in their original 1993 work when they wrote, "None of the management fads of the last twenty years—not management by objectives, diversification, Theory Z, zero-based budgeting, value chain analysis, decentralization, quality circles, 'excellence,' restructuring, portfolio management, management by walking around, matrix management, intrapreneuring, or one-minute managing—has reversed the deterioration of America's corporate competitive performance. They have only distracted managers from the real task at hand." Yet, in spite of that original warning and its later repetition, managements of poorly performing companies viewed "reengineering" as yet another infallible theory that would put everything right. It doesn't, as Hammer and Champy would be the first to agree. On the contrary, where reengineering has been viewed as a business *system*, rather than as a *goal*, it has failed as surely as every other system has, just as Hammer warned it surely would.

The astounding rise in billings by management consultants of all types during the last decade illustrates American management's hunger for support. Where fearless entrepreneurial spirit is lacking, the people in charge need a crutch instead. Today, an estimated 80,000 management consulting professionals in the United States and abroad are providing dubious management expertise to an excessive and dangerous degree.

Obviously, many consultants provide real expertise. For example, the main task of many of the studies conducted by the large accounting firms' consultancies is to install appropriate bookkeeping and management information systems, and the software that goes with them. In such instances, management is actually buying know-how, not consulting advice. As long as the purveyor of the know-how actually knows how, this is money well spent. But in large measure, management retains consultants to advise on how to organize for success. And therefore what the consultants recommend is their system for achieving success. For the most part, those systems don't work. The sad fact is that this still explosively growing consulting industry was largely (although, fortunately, not entirely) based upon a false premise: the dangerously wrongheaded notion that excellence in business (or for that matter in educational or in political organizations) depends on getting the technique right by mimicking the structure of other successful businesses.

Surprised by the appearance of fleet-footed foreign competitors in their once exclusive markets, American executives were looking for simple answers and fast results. Because, as Peters assured his readers, the world's best companies were American, it followed that the best of American companies were by far the best in the world. Thus, all American managers had to do to shake off the threat of foreign competitors was to copy the organizational structure of America's most "excellent" companies. Like P. T. Barnum, the consultants—with Peters prominent among them—gave the people what they wanted.

But of course this is where Peters and his willing audience went so terribly wrong. The root of excellence in organizations, whether they have a business, educational, or political focus, is not structure—it is *people*. As Hammer and Champy put it, "Companies don't reengineer processes; people do."

If nothing else, the collapse of communism proved that management by bureaucracy, as distinct from management by achieving individuals, just plain doesn't work. Clearly defined management hierarchies in the U.S.S.R. produced neither adequate material goods nor even a fulfilling bureaucratic life. Communism's stifling of Adam Smith's "invisible hand" led to horrendous shortages of basic goods and a painfully ineffective welfare state that punished most of its citizens every day of their lives.

We must quickly admit, however, that in one respect we are being somewhat unfair to Peters and Waterman. They are an easy target because they made such clear statements and thus could be shown to be so clearly wrong. But they were not alone. On the contrary, as I have already emphasized, they merely epitomize the errors made by most consulting groups and business gurus, each of whom developed a theory of business that they claimed provided *the* real and complete solutions. The ideas were presented as if business responded to immutable natural laws and could therefore be run simply by applying them.

Theories based on Japanese practice have now been debunked as Japan's economy, artificially pumped up by government support that helped generate huge paper profits in real estate, has collapsed to realistic levels. The Boston Consulting Group's theory, spruced up with zippy catchphrases such as "cash cows," has been recognized for what it is, merely a simple (and not even always correct) contention that the market leader has an economic advantage over the followers. It was, of course, a finding largely unaccompanied by any prescription for actually achieving such leadership. The implementation of reengineering (although not what Hammer advocated) has been unveiled to be, in most cases, little more than cost-cutting handled without much finesse. And the same sort of criticisms can be leveled at most of the other ideas peddled over the last decade by business consultants of many stripes.

Moreover, it is not only our popular gurus and consulting firms that have sought to perpetuate the myth that there are "immutable" theories of business akin to, say, the immutable theories of physics (which themselves are, of course, not immutable either). Our great universities, with Harvard, Wharton, and Stanford in the vigorous vanguard, have trumpeted the view that business laws exist and can be taught. And, no doubt, using clever cases and experienced teachers, many business "tricks of the trade" can be imparted to bright students. I hope that University of Southern California students emerged from my courses a little more prepared to deal with the "slings and arrows of (always) outrageous fortune" that they will encounter as they run their own entrepreneurial ventures or join someone else's start-up. But teaching know-how, is a long way from the idea that there are *laws* of management structure, or that they can be formulated and taught. Indeed, the latest generation of business school students is beginning to see this shortcoming for what it is. Enrollment (or the waiting lists for enrollment) in business schools is declining. Only the classes teaching entrepreneurialism, where no theoretical construct is even claimed, are growing. Budding entrepreneurs know they have a lot to learn about the methods of building businesses. But they know too that no one will pretend to the existence of an overall set of laws, a sort of General Theory of business. The only immutable law of business I know is that there is no such theory.

The opportunities for both big and small businesses are greater than ever. But so are the risks. International competition has turned ferocious. The Asian economists are self-destructing. Unfriendly takeovers (or "friendly" ones forced on unwary managers) are rampant. The barriers between countries have largely fallen, and new competitors from Europe and Latin America are emerging like beasts from the darkness, both to invade the American economy, and to capture what we have rather arrogantly called "American markets" abroad. For many battered executives, the 1990s may seem like a frightening return to the Darwinian free-for-all that best describes the America of the Rockefellers and the Vanderbilts, or the Napoleonic Europe of the first Rothschilds, long before the comfortable government-regulated pleasantries of modern business had been established.

At this very moment, heads are rolling in some of the greatest companies in America because their owners have not "downsized" fast enough. If you are a CEO, there is nothing wrong, it seems, with firing 10,000 employees you hired unnecessarily and taking a one-time loss of several hundred million dollars. That, we are told, is tough and intelligent business thinking. But woe to those few executives who didn't hire anyone unnecessarily and laid off people sensibly and gradually as efficiencies improved. If they insist that they should therefore keep their staffs intact, ride out some small competitor-induced business slowdown, and use their well-trained employees to fight back and regain the initiative, they will be chopped down mercilessly—and never vindicated even though the upturn comes and they are proven right.

Downsizing is definitely not the inevitable answer when a business faces trouble. Sometimes, of course, it may be necessary as a correction of earlier errors. In that case, I contend that the first candidates for the "downsizing" should be the management who made those errors initially.

All too frequently, we find some giant ship of commerce listing with discarded ideas that seemed appealing in their time but had to be thrown out because they were based on the false premise that universally applicable business laws exist. They do not, and it's time to clear the decks and begin again. It is high time we really understand what lies behind this seductive idea of excellence.

BUSINESS DOES *NOT* FOLLOW NATURAL LAWS

Excellence in business does not happen merely because you get the structure right. Excellence springs only from human effort, from the human mind, from the human heart. Excellence is a work of human hands, and thought, and intuition. And excellence can *only* be personal. Not every member of any group is "excellent." In the sight of God, we may all be equally important, and in our democracy we should all be given an equal chance to shine. There is nothing wrong with affirmative action except that it kicks in when people are already too old; at the beginning of learning, kids who are behind in knowledge but innately intelligent can catch up. Later, affirmative action puts people into jobs they cannot handle and is therefore counterproductive. However, even if we succeed in giving everyone an equal chance, in practice only very few and rare people will turn out to be real "exceptional individuals," gifted with the talent and the desire to get things done. Most people, regardless of their education and training, just don't have a talent for achievement, just as most people, regardless of how long they practice, will never play the violin like Heifetz or dunk a basketball like Shaq.

Excellence in business (or in any other institution) must begin with those rare and special individuals who *are* able to carry a new idea forward into the boardroom, the workplace, or the marketplace, and *get it done*. In the process, those excellent people will get the structure of their companies right, just as they will make sure that the machines in their factories work. Each of those structures will be different, of course. And to try to install any one of them, however effective it was where it was originally used, into another set of business circumstances would be as absurd as to try to dribble a football or slam-dunk a touchdown. Many companies have forgotten this simple truth, at the vast expense of themselves, their laid-off and demoralized workers, and their embattled shareholders.

These special, excellent people with the talent for getting things done, apparently forgotten by many businesses, are nevertheless the essential fuel that drives all commerce. Moreover, as I shall discuss later, these are not only the people who drive businesses—they are truly the people who drive the world. These are the people this book seeks to identify, define, and describe. Admittedly, they may not be working for the good of anyone but their own companies. They may or may not believe in Engine Charlie Wilson's almost forgotten 1950s claim that what is good for General Motors is good for the country, and they may or may not care. But Wilson was right in principle (if not necessarily about GM). Adam Smith wrote in *The Wealth of Nations* that "it is not from benevolence of the butcher, the brewer, or the baker that we expect our dinner, but from their regard to their own interest." Thus, whatever their motivation, businesspeople do "do good." Moreover, I am sure that there is more to it than mere inevitability: in fact, companies with products as disparate as the Body Shop, a cosmetics retailer, and Ben & Jerry's, an ice cream manufacturer, both directly support protection of the rain forest. Whether they do it out of the goodness of their heart or because it is good advertising is, of course, open to question. But it hardly matters, since, either way, the good is done.

The principle of the division of labor, enunciated by Adam Smith, implemented by Henry Ford, and organized by Alfred Sloan (and, of course, by many others at each step) is giving way to a new paradigm, one that is not yet clearly defined. All we do know is that knowledge cannot be broken into bits as easily as can production-line manufacturing. Indeed, for a knowledge worker, combining knowledge may be far more efficient than splitting it. Nevertheless, Smith's overall principle, namely that the invisible hand of profit will inevitably cause business to do whatever is most cost effective, continues to pertain. In fact, it is that very principle that is causing the shift in businesspeople's behavior in context with computers, the Internet, and all the other new tools of knowledge now available to us. That shift, which lies at the heart of the fundamental change in business we see all over the world (and which I shall discuss in detail later), places *more* emphasis on the individual, and particularly on the overachieving individual, than ever before. This new era could well be called the Age of the Individual. Thus, it is far more than a "good thing"; it is indeed a life-saver that even where businesspeople do not *intend* to do good—and even if their drive to build businesses is purely selfish—there can be no reasonable doubt that, willy-nilly, they do.

This book, then, is my personal examination of those special folk in business who make things happen. It is my personal, pragmatic, maverick view, based not on psychological research or controlled clinical experimentation but on the drives and experiences of my business friends and associates. This book does not depend merely on theory for, although I have certainly researched such theory as it exists, little is applicable. Rather, it is based on my close observation of how business leaders actually behave, how they run, and even why. In net, it elucidates my views on the ethology of the "movers and shakers" of business.

Thus, *The Exceptional Individual* is more than a recipe for achievement, although it includes that. Rather, its thesis is that excellence springs from certain individuals who embody it and give it life, and that these men and women have a certain set of attributes that may be identified and attitudes that may be encouraged and thus enhanced.

I wish to explore how achievers bowl over obstacles, institute new ways of doing things, or find ways to turn business reverses to advantage. This book includes some familiar faces you will know from the financial pages, like Henry Kravitz, Bill Gates, and H. Ross Perot, but mostly it relies on more specific examples drawn from my own business experience. For the vital fact that I have discovered over decades of experience of working with hundreds of different companies is that *the people who make things happen are scattered throughout successful organizations.* They are not necessarily in the limelight. They are by no means only CEOs and owners.

Rather, they crop up at all levels and in all areas of successful firms. James C. Collins and Jerry I. Porras are right when they state unequivocally that "just about *anyone* can be a key protagonist in building an extraordinary business institution," although they go overboard when they expand this to suggest that everyone can "make things happen." Certainly, training and encouragement nourish potential achievers to perform up to their full potential. But the talent for achievement must also be there. Some people have it; many simply don't.

I have set my sights high in this book: *The Exceptional Individual* is designed to be both instructive and a good read. I shall be successful, however, just as businesspeople are, only when finite results are achieved. *The Exceptional Individual* will enable you to identify those driven men and women who feel the need for change more than they feel the need for the safety of the status quo. They are absolutely necessary to business and must be recruited, encouraged, and rewarded. I am confident that these principles I shall present in this book will help you in a practical way, by learning how to recognize, encourage, and challenge those people in your organization who are capable of real achievement. After all, the role they play is vital to the success of your business.

I have been writing about this subject for many years. Indeed, in 1976 I wrote a book called *The Overachievers*. In it I expressed many of the ideas, and even used some of the words, that I am repeating here. But my thinking then was not as clear; I had less experience, and *the harm some consultants caused had only just started to occur.* Hindsight is twenty-twenty, and I realize now that American business must rethink itself from the ground up to continue to survive and prosper in the face of ever-strengthening competition from all over the world. It must do so bearing one simple, funda-

mental, frequently forgotten truth in mind: Certain key individuals, those rare, risk-taking, dynamic, creative, and
driven people we often call entrepreneurs, provide the solution, the *only* solution, to all our business problems. These
are the people whom I formerly dubbed the overachievers.
They were the ones who built America's economy during its
early, cowboy days; who built its railroads, struck its oil,
founded its retail system, established its manufacturing, built
its cars. Later, these entrepreneurs built our airlines, our television industry, our health industry. Those are the entrepreneurs who built our modern-day computers, genetic
medicine, our revolutionary start at bioengineering, our incredible communications explosion, and all the rest of the
mind-boggling new vistas opening up before us.

As I shall discuss in the final chapter of this book, we are
fortunate to be living in the midst of a step forward in the
evolution of humanity so large that it is actually visible to
the naked eye. As *Newsweek* put it in their July 31, 1995,
issue, "We are witnessing an epochal moment in American
sociology, the birth of a new class." *Newsweek* calls those people the Overclass and defines them as a class of people that
"values competitive achievement." They are my "Exceptional Individuals," those members of *Newsweek*'s Overclass.
Of course, being individuals, they obviously do not constitute
a class at all. Rather, they are wonderful overachievers who,
like their forebears, use the latest technologies and exploit
the latest opportunities to get things done. *Newsweek* lists a
hundred of them. It's an impressive list of achievers—and a
fabulous list of achievements. Even so, I believe *Newsweek*
*under*estimates the degree of change. It is far more than a
sociological change, I suggest, and is in fact more akin to an
evolutionary one. In any case, whether the change is
"merely" epochal or is, indeed, seminal, on one point *News-*

week and I completely agree: the change is powered by those "exceptional individuals" about whom this book is written.

We undervalue them, these high-achieving entrepreneurs. We do not know enough about how to find them, nurture them, encourage them, and then bask in the advantages they bring us. This book will help redress that wrong. Above all, it is intended to fuel your desire for improvement—and motivate you to *action*.

As a reader, you may well agree that excellence in business can be learned or acquired, or at the very least enhanced. You or your company may profit from these insights by using them to hire and promote wisely. You may sharpen your self-understanding. You may more easily identify excellence in the workplace. As an individual involved in business, you may even become more personally successful when you recognize the power of these simple but fundamental ideas.

As Plato observed, knowledge is power.

2

CHALLENGING THE STARS

The best business organizations, like soaring rockets, challenge the stars. H. Ross Perot's Electronic Data Systems, Sam Walton's Wal-Mart, Bill Gates's Microsoft Corporation, and, earlier, Ray Kroc's McDonald's, and countless other companies, all seemed to rise on the wings of their creators' visions. Quite a few, like Procter & Gamble, General Electric, and Philip Morris, continue to orbit high above the mundane level of ordinary corporations, apparently forever. (P&G has continued its success virtually unabated since 1837; Philip Morris has since 1847; and GE, the newcomer, since 1892.)

But the worst of business organizations, like Charles Keating's Lincoln Savings and Loan, Carl Icahn's TWA, Michael Milkin's Drexel, Burnham Lambert, Campeau's Federated Department Stores, and the overleveraged real estate empire of the Reichmans in Toronto, seemed to rise high for a moment but then career to an inevitable crash. Some, like TWA, revive—only to fail again and rise again in a continuous cycle of the Perils of Pauline. Occasionally some of these organizations, for example, IBM, rise again to new heights of sustainable success. But too often they first pass through bankruptcy, leaving behind them massive unpaid debts. To call such revivals successes is to redefine the word and trivialize further the already rocky concept of fiscal honor.

Of course a majority of companies neither achieve the lasting greatness of a Procter & Gamble or Disney, nor do they collapse under their own weight. While Procter & Gamble soars, Lever plods. While General Electric sets new records, Westinghouse has trouble matching its own prior ones. While Disney goes from strength to strength, the rest of the film industry seems to struggle from merger to merger.

Can the difference, then, between the great, the mediocre, and the awful be traced back solely to the difference in the achievement potential of their leaders?

Of course not. Companies that have existed for decades, in many cases over a hundred years, cannot ascribe their excellence to the coincidence of having a constant string of superb CEOs, significantly better than the CEOs of their lackluster rivals. This is the point made eloquently (if a trifle lengthily!) by James Collins and Jerry Porras in their fine 1994 book, *Built to Last*. They compare "visionary companies," that is, those that have had clear superiority over all their rivals for a very long time, with a set of comparable companies that are similar in all respects except long-lasting excellence. For example, they point out that 3M, a "visionary" company by almost anyone's standards, has had ten CEOs since its founding in 1904, and that many of them were hardly "visionary" leaders. They further show that "3M could not possibly trace its success primarily to a visionary product concept, market insight, or lucky break." This too seems perfectly obvious.

Then to what do 3M, Procter & Gamble, Philip Morris, and the other visionary companies Collins and Porras describe owe their superiority? Here is the answer they derived from their exhaustive studies: "The visionary companies did a better job than the comparison companies at developing and promoting highly competent managerial talent from inside the company, and thereby attained greater continuity of their excellence." For example, they point out that while Welch is no doubt a remarkable leader of General Electric, he is neither the first that company has selected nor likely to be the last. "Somehow GE *the organization* had the ability to attract, retain, develop, groom, and select Welch the leader," they write. "The selection of Welch stemmed from a good corporate architecture."

Collins and Porras correctly emphasize that "you don't have to accept the false view that, until your company has a charismatic visionary leader, it cannot become a visionary company." Rather, they repeat again and again, you need to be "an *organizational* visionary and build an environment where *everyone* has the opportunity to exceed, to take the initiative, to *achieve. . . . The continuity of superb individuals atop visionary companies stems from the companies being outstanding organizations, not the other way around,*" they conclude. (Both the breathlessness and the italics are theirs!)

I concur with almost every word Collins and Porras write in their book. But the operative word in that last sentence is *almost*. For there is one telling point that they miss. It is that there is no such thing as an "organization." There is only a group of people working together. "Organization" is an abstract principle. *People* are the reality behind that principle. Among those people, some are high achievers, some are facilitators (i.e. the implementers who help the achievers get their work done as I shall discuss later), and most are merely drones who do little more than clog the system. Organizations that, for one reason or another, have attracted many high achievers are effective and exciting. As a result, they are able to attract many more. And *that* is why they remain in the vanguard and are viewed by Collins and Porras, and indeed by most of us, as visionary.

For it remains unarguably certain that neither a business nor a rocket can lift off its launching pad, keep climbing once it is launched, or maintain itself in orbit over time without some form of controlled but explosive energy. That energy, the "rocket fuel" of business, is the vigor, daring, and ability of certain very special men and women. They may be chief executive officers of Fortune 500 companies. They may be middle management, brilliantly maneuvering their way up through the ranks. Most assuredly, however, they are neither reading nor thinking about the precepts enunciated in a book written by an acquaintance of mine, *How to Be a Successful Middle Manager*. Their drive is for success by performance, not process. If they are not employed by "big" business, they may be launching their first or second small business. However, wherever they are, they are sure to be creating action where there was none. Imperceptibly at first, the company or division or tiny department stirs under their influence; then, apparently miraculously motivated, it blasts off to nearly unbelievable achievement.

About fifteen years ago a little Brooklyn food company was teetering on the edge of bankruptcy. Its products were good, its organization was strong, but consumers outside metropolitan New York knew little about its brands. The top officials of the company believed in their products. A few years previously, they had tried television advertising. The results had been great, but the company had been unable to finance the campaign beyond the test market area. The project was dropped. Sales were weak and eroding under the increasing pressure of stronger, TV-advertised competitors.

Somewhere in a back room sat a very young man earning the grand sum of $24,000 annually. He was trying hard to cultivate a mustache in order to look older, and perhaps to compensate for the fact that, in spite of his youth, he was starting to lose his hair. His title was media manager. He had been hired merely to place a few trade ads and an occasional consumer ad in newspaper food pages and food-related magazines.

Our young hero's position was hardly an exalted one from which to save the firm. Yet save it he did. Sitting there in his little back room, he recognized the advent of cable television and realized that the cable channels would soon need a variety of new, specialized programs to fill their airtime. All alone, he created several simple television shows, developed the ideas, wrote the words. He learned the techniques of scripting and presentation from a TV script reader who was also his girlfriend. He located a writer of cookbooks who agreed to host his shows for a small fee and the chance to build an audience for her publishing career. When he was finished, he had some simple, inexpensive cooking programs ready for production.

Still without informing management, he bartered the company's shows with start-up cable companies in return for advertising time and the small amount of cash he needed to produce them. He used the advertising time to promote the company's products. In effect, he had succeeded in obtaining advertising for nothing.

As the cable industry grew, the small Brooklyn company's food shows became more popular. Its advertising became more and more effective, in regional, national, and then even international markets. Today that food company is many times the size it was. It is highly profitable—and run by a tough-minded, $300,000-a-year, totally bald ex–media man!

The type of people who provide the rocket fuel for industry are of peculiar and rare talent. Often they face tremendous opposition. More often than not, they are forced to overcome a depressing inertia that surrounds them. Sometimes they destroy their health, although they are healthy and hyperenergetic as a rule. While they typically work like dogs, they are not "workaholics." That term applies to people who harm their lives by working too obsessively. On the contrary, true "exceptional individuals" love the work they do, and thrive on it. Usually they are gifted with humor and sound intelligence. Typically, they are people who, with Thoreau, hear "a different drummer" and have the courage to "step to the music" they hear.

These men and women are logical business thinkers and have trained themselves to consider the available facts before they make a decision. But their own behavior often exceeds logic. Their iconoclastic dissatisfaction with static institutions, their gut-tearing need to get things moving, to improve every enterprise, cannot easily be explained. Sometimes their personal determination for improvement, their scorn for the "path of least resistance," seems to transcend the rational. It stems from some inner need that allows them to achieve more than other equally knowledgeable, bright people.

These are the obverse of those "underachievers" who accomplish less than their ability suggests they should. Underachievers are a well-known educational phenomenon, defined by the Department of Health and Human Services as people with "superior ability . . . whose performance . . . is significantly below their measured or demonstrated aptitudes or potential for academic achievement." Such underachievement is not explained by major physical illness or serious psychological upset, although those factors certainly affect achievement. Rather, underachievers are people who do not do as well as they should by all predictive criteria. How many of us used to receive report cards from school that said something like "Could do better if he tried" or "Not working up to her potential"? That is underachievement—

although I often wonder whether it is the underachievement of the child or the teacher!

The elusive spirit that drives people is not easily explicable. I believe the drive to achieve is a virtue or a vice (depending on your point of view) that is inborn or developed very early in life. Certainly, it is an aptitude that may be fostered and nurtured, but I doubt whether it can be created. Some people have a talent for song and others for solitude. Some paint, others write poetry, still others play tennis with uncanny skill. As Homer put it in the *Iliad*, "To one man a God has given deeds of war, and to another the dance, to another the lyre and song, and in another wise-sounding Zeus puts a good mind." Some people are thus endowed with a talent for "getting things done" in the business, and they have an inner compulsion to devote themselves to doing just that. When that drive is combined with the determination to inspire a similar spirit in others, the combination becomes irresistible.

Former army intelligence officer Sam Walton began his first Wal-Mart in 1962, in the unlikely small, overly hot backwater of Bentonville, Arkansas. But Walton's drive, coupled with the enthusiasm he engendered in his "associates," as he called his employees, built Wal-Mart into an empire of 1,700 low-priced retail stores with over $45 billion in sales, and made Wal-Mart the leading retailer in America.

His competitors constantly underestimated this hokey hillbilly who once did the hula on Wall Street when he lost a wager. What they saw was merely a plain-spoken man who drove a beat-up pickup truck. They decided he was a small-town retailer who would achieve limited, regional success: Good luck to him!

Indeed, Sam Walton's basic idea was simple, even simplistic.

Namely, it was to take the discount-store concept into towns with populations of less than 50,000 that discounters like Kmart and Target believed were too small to support such large stores. It was not even an original idea. Ames Stores had been started about four years earlier on the same concept. But, as one of Sam Walton's biographers, Vance Trimble, wrote, "Other retailers were out there trying to do just what he was doing. Only he did it better than nearly anyone." Actually, I believe he did it better than everyone because he was able to operate more efficiently than any of his rivals. That may have been partly because he used many new technologies for greater operating efficiency. For example, he pioneered the use of computers and satellite technology to link sales data from individual stores with suppliers, thereby allowing them to tailor their production to Wal-Mart's needs and reduce inventory costs.

However, probably the main reason for Sam Walton's success was that he created an environment in which everyone at Wal-Mart was encouraged to "overachieve." This plan, designed to bring out the best in Wal-Mart people, characterized the firm from its inception. Very soon after it started, Walton began profit-sharing with even his lower-level employees. Eventually, many of them became rich. He shared each store's sales figures with his associates, something few managers would do, and used the numbers as the basis for weekly meetings that critiqued Wal-Mart operations. He encouraged his employees to run their departments as if they were their own businesses. He created the concept of volume producing items (VIPs) to encourage associates to experiment with product merchandising. He publicly featured employees whose experiments worked. As a result, he generated extraordinary enthusiasm among his employees as he personally led them in the corny but still exhilarating Wal-Mart cheer.

Later, of course, and to this day, small merchants complained bitterly about Wal-Mart, whining to 60 Minutes that they were

24

being "forced" out of business because they could not buy as efficiently as the giant retailer. But Sam Walton ran just one small store when he started. He inherited nothing special, no mandated advantage over all his competitors. They could have done what he did. The simple fact is, they didn't—and all the whining in the world cannot rectify that oversight now that it is too late.

On paper, Sam Walton seemed to be a very ordinary fellow. Certainly, he drove himself hard. Whether working or relaxing by training bird dogs, hunting quail, and playing tennis, he always showed a fierce competitive spirit. But nothing in his résumé, appearance, or behavior would have predicted that he would generate a personal fortune of billions. That he did attests to the power of the people he encouraged around him to become impressive achievers of extraordinary results.

As far back as 1977 an article in the *Discount Merchandiser* noted that Sam Walton had created an organization that encouraged achievers. His rivals had not. For example, the Gilman brothers, who founded Ames, never achieved anywhere near Walton's success because they prescribed to the last detail what each store manager had to do, and therefore left no room for personal achievement—or the individuals likely to strive for it.

At first glance, there appears to be no behavioral, physical, educational, national, age, religious, or gender standard for those rare individuals who succeed so much more dramatically than one could predict. They have backgrounds of infinite variety. They are naturally all intelligent, but their intelligence varies from merely above average to near genius. Their appearance may vary from attractive to ugly, upright to hunchbacked—although they never lack vigor and drive.

Their personalities may vary from ebullient to introverted. They create movement in many different directions. Certainly their methods of achievement are infinitely various.

A few months after he took over as Chrysler's CEO, I set up a meeting between Lee Iacocca, whom I knew through a close mutual friend, and another friend of mine who wanted to make a complicated barter deal to acquire a fleet of cars. It was well known that Chrysler had thousands of excess cars standing unsalable in inventory.

The meeting took place in Lee's giant suite in New York's Waldorf Towers hotel, just the three of us seated in the middle of a room large enough to be approached with a six-iron. My friend, Fred, explained what he wanted to arrange. Lee became raptly interested. After a few minutes, I began to worry about his obvious fascination. Was he expecting a much larger order than my friend Fred could manage?

"Tell me, Lee," I interrupted nervously, "how many cars are you thinking about? I mean, what would be a"—I hesitated, looking for the right description—"an appropriate, say, average order."

The answer shot back at me: "Four."

Now I was really confused. Did he mean four dozen, four hundred, four thousand? "You mean four, er . . ."

Lee Iacocca (I Am Chairman of Chrysler Corporation of America) looked at me coldly. "I mean," he said distinctly. "I would be pleased to sell this gentleman four effing cars!" Except he used no such euphemism.

Lee Iacocca pulled Chrysler Corporation from the brink of financial ruin through evangelical salesmanship. Just as George Romney had saved American Motors in the 1960s by taunting Detroit for making "gas-guzzling monsters," so Iacocca convinced the world of Chrysler's place in the vanguard of automotive excellence.

Then he sold the U.S. Congress on the idea of bailing Chrysler out of debt, and sold a skeptical Wall Street on the company's staying power. Amazingly, he succeeded in scooping water out of the company's leaky boat for so long that Chrysler was actually able to catch up and fulfill the promises he made. Along the way, before he formally retired, Iacocca wrote one of the best-selling business books of the 1980s, and headed a successful fund-raising effort to restore the Statue of Liberty and Ellis Island where his own Italian ancestors and many millions of immigrants like them first understood that America was the land of individual *opportunity. Here, you were free to achieve to whatever extent you could.*

Romney and Iacocca were supersalesmen who, like Ross Perot earlier and Bill Gates today, stood out as charismatic icons. However, "exceptional individuals" come in many different varieties.

In 1965, Gordon Moore, the founder of Intel, whom BusinessWeek *has nominated as ''the folk hero of American capitalism,'' predicted that the power of silicon chips would increase exponentially. He was correct, for today's four-megabyte chip is about five million times more powerful than the transistors that existed then. Moore wrote that, as a result, ''electronic techniques [will be] . . . generally available throughout all of society.'' As the expression goes, he sure got that one right!*

But although he was a scientist, he was not at all content with merely making forecasts. Indeed, he was fond of boasting that it was the scientists, not the student protestors marching outside their laboratories, who were the genuine revolutionaries. Again, he saw the truth. While the mainframe makers refused to see the inevitable drop in the price of computing—or, like IBM, saw it but initially reacted only with great reluctance—Gordon Moore and his partner Robert Noyce built Intel into the megacorporation it is today.

As BusinessWeek *described him, Gordon Moore never swore or made disparaging comments about people. Almost the quintessential nice guy, Gordon Moore in no way matches today's popular image of the "hard-driving businessman." Yet, in 1957, it was largely under Moore's influence that he and seven others left William Shockley's semiconductor company to start Fairchild Semiconductor—because Shockley was moving too slowly. It was again Moore who, ten years later, joined Robert Noyce in starting Intel—because Fairchild was moving too slowly. And it was Moore who took over the top spot of Intel in 1979 when the whole thing became a bit too much for Bob Noyce. "If you slow down, you really doom yourself," Moore explained. "Pulling back is the road to disaster."*

Just as surely as George Romney and Lee Iacocca saved their car companies, Alfred Sloan saved General Motors a few decades earlier. In his book, *My Years With General Motors,* Mr. Sloan wrote that General Motors "at the close of the year 1920 . . . faced simultaneously an economic slump on the outside and a management crisis on the inside." It was his "organization study" that "served the purpose" of turning General Motors around, Sloan writes in magnificent understatement. The company recovered brilliantly.

However, although Alfred Sloan was a genius of administration, this is not the most impressive thing about his book. The really surprising thing is that he never sought to lift his organizational approach to the level of theory. What he did for GM was right for GM at the time, he believed. And he was right on. But in the midst of talking about his new organization, his real and constant emphasis was on *implementation*, on getting things done. There was apparently never the thought in his mind that his method had some sort of universality to it, that if you organized à la Sloan you would succeed. Rather, he organized simply to get the job done. "The divisions naturally resisted this move . . . but I persuaded them," he writes of one idea. (Being "persuaded" by Mr. Sloan must have been an energizing experience!) The point is that for GM, *at that time*, an organizational hierarchy was what was needed. Sloan would never have assumed that such concentration on organization would be a permanent answer.

In the final sentence of his book, Sloan wrote, "The work of creating goes on." However, sadly, this proved not to be the case. Future generations of managers and CEOs forgot that Sloan viewed administrative structure as merely a means to an end. Instead they elevated that structure into a whole business theory, equating it, rather than its achievements, with excellence. They thus squandered a good part of their market share to increasingly aggressive competitors from around the world who were not inhibited by a "structure" that had become suddenly top-heavy. Only very recently has a new generation of management recognized that action, not methodology, leads to success. With that recognition, GM has undergone a most impressive turnaround.

The right people—and often just one single individual—is what is needed to create business success. Such a person with the "right stuff" for business can achieve the well nigh impossible.

While Sloan was reorganizing General Motors, on the other side of the world in prewar Japan, the relentlessly energetic Soichiro Honda was so busy learning about engines and repairing them that he didn't even qualify for a degree at a technical school. Nearly killed in a racing accident, Honda gave up his dream of becoming a race driver and turned his attention to manufacturing. Honda's *small manufacturing plant was bombed into ruin during World War II, but in 1948 he spent $1,500 for 500 small engines he bought from military surplus and got a crew to fasten them to bicycles. He was soon making his own small engines. At the outset, they ran on pine-resin fuel because gasoline was rationed. Honda expanded so fast that, by 1958, he was selling a million motorcycles a year. Honda made a virtue of continuous learning and teamwork, to vastly accelerate product cycles and dramatically improve quality. Then, in 1962, he used that know-how to enter the auto industry. His first car was small and unattractive, and the incumbent American auto giants chuckled. Then, as Honda's share started to grow, they tried to copy Japanese methodology. Before long, Honda became the best-selling car in the United States, and the American auto industry started generating extraordinary losses.*

Consultants, reviewing the American automotive companies and comparing them to Honda's operation, had a field day. Too bad it wasn't an American success strategy! But never mind; if you couldn't praise Yankee ingenuity, you could vilify American stodginess instead. That was almost as good. Dozens of books about Japanese teamwork began to emerge, and Detroit started talking about "total quality." None of this helped. Not until the end of the 1980s did matters change—in two respects. On the one hand, Detroit started remembering that quality counts. From the ground up, a new generation of "exceptional individuals" began cutting costs, "downsizing" bureaucracies— and building better cars. On the other hand, the Japanese, perhaps overimpressed by the management gurus who were extolling the virtues of Japanese methodology, started to forget the basics. Soichiro Honda retired as others of his generation also retired or died. They were replaced by functionaries. "From autocrat to bureaucrat," as a friend of mine summarized. The result: Detroit's world market share rose; Japan's fell.

WHAT DO THEY HAVE IN COMMON?

Although overachievers operate in vastly different ways, there are similarities in their psychological makeup. In 1964, Collins, Moore, and Unwalla concluded that one of the similarities was that entrepreneurs (whom they defined as high achievers) suffered (or, I suppose, benefited) from unresolved Oedipal problems—which sounds pretty silly to me!

More interesting are the views of the earlier and more sensible economists who were mostly working businesspeople themselves and, with few exceptions, achievers of impressive credentials. Thus, between about 1915 and about 1930, Max Weber ascribed achievement by entrepreneurs largely to the "Protestant Work Ethic." This, he explained, was why entrepreneurial achievement was really only to be found in Western civilization. (I have always wondered how he would have explained the modern capitalist hotbeds of the Pacific Rim.) Weber is important because he influenced so many of his fellow historians and economists of the period, including Joseph Schumpeter. Writing in *The Journal of Economic History* with his normal mixture of clear insight and turgid prose, Schumpeter declared that "it took an individual who possessed the unusual traits and will to found a private kingdom, a drive to overcome obstacles, a joy in creating, and satisfaction in exercising one's ingenuity to become an entrepreneur." And it was the job of that entrepreneur, as Schumpeter had explained much earlier, "to carry out new combinations of production," a function that was fundamental to modern economic development. "His" entrepreneur is the "exceptional individual" I am now addressing.

The fact of the matter is that, whatever theorists we admire, none have adequately described the commonality among high achievers. However, we do know that these achievers have something in common. For while this trait is hard to describe, it is as obvious as light to the naked eye. While it is true that a firefly is nothing like a fluorescent light and that neither is similar to the moon, they all glow. In that one key respect, then, they are similar. "Exceptional individuals" "glow" in many different ways, but always to a degree that exceeds the glow of ordinary people "as great'st does least," in the words of Shakespeare. Indeed, some of them have such raw talent for achievement that, even without any particular hunger for success, they cannot fail to attain a bit of it. Eventually, they may become "hungry" too—and then, of course, they blast off to glory.

An amusing example of this is the story of a brilliant young woman who wanted to "drop out" in her youth. But success dogged her footsteps. After high school she left home to live in Guatemala, where she survived for a year making beautiful, hand-painted dolls. But finally, hounded by her family to return to school, she took a degree in business.

Straight out of college, this capable young woman accepted a job in sales with a plastic sheeting company. Apparently she fell into the situation as a result of some contacts provided by her family, without caring much one way or the other. Nevertheless, within only three years, she had parlayed her job from simple salesperson to ownership of a substantial sales franchise company representing one of the billion-dollar plastics concerns. She had sales offices and salespeople all over the United States and was well on her way to becoming a millionaire. Then she gave this all away, impetuously and uncaringly, to her estranged husband. Happy to be rid of her success (and, I assume, her husband), she then became the janitor of an apartment building. As she explained, it left her leisure time to read.

To her chagrin, she was quickly promoted to building manager—with no time to read! ''I had no alternative but to quit,'' she explained.

When the money she had saved was gone, she went to work for Macy's as a stock clerk. ''I thought it would be fun to drive the forklift,'' she said.

But within days she was promoted to sales assistant. Bored to tears with standing behind the counter, she soon decided, for her own amusement, to put on her own private sales drive. For three consecutive weeks she achieved the highest individual sales in the Macy's chain. Inevitably she was promoted to junior buyer, no closer to her ambition of dropping out.

Determined as this young woman was, she quit this job. This time she joined a small advertising agency as a mail runner. ''If they won't let me drive a forklift, at least I can run around in the open air with never a care or a worry,'' she rationalized.

Unfortunately, within two weeks, she opened her mouth to criticize some advertising she was to deliver, and came up with a better version. ''I should have bitten my tongue off,'' she said.

And so she was elevated again, this time to junior copywriter. And then, within less than a year, to account executive and finally, meteorically, to vice president. ''They sent me to Harvard to study how to be the success I desperately didn't want to be!'' she exclaimed. ''So I decided, after all, to seek success. I decided to go for it.''

Once she had made that decision, she worked with zeal. She

achieved enormous feats, but her enthusiasm lasted only a year or so and finally her drive for underachievement got the better of her. She left to go back to a small private university as an undergraduate in a field she had never studied. ''Surely in academe I shall be able to find a way to do practically nothing,'' she reasoned. The field she chose was arcane, a literary backwater dealing with the deconstruction of medieval French poetry.

The last I heard of her she had earned her Ph.D. and become an assistant professor whose classes were crowded to capacity.

Achievers exist in every field of human endeavor, not just in business. And they change our lives in fundamental ways. For all the prate and prattle we have become accustomed to hearing from our politicians, many of them are wonderfully effective in getting things done. Following the California earthquake of early 1994, the newly elected mayor, Richard Riordan, quietly arranged to pay incentives to builders who could get the damaged freeway overpasses repaired quickly. Within weeks, the city's traffic was running freely again. (It took longer to get bureaucratic approval to repair the chimney on a house I owned than it took the mayor to fix the road system!)

Among the most impressive of political overachievers, a man who most certainly achieved more than his demeanor, apparent intellect, or credentials would lead you to have anticipated, is former President Ronald Reagan. I am not discussing here whether what he set out to do was right; I am merely commenting on his extraordinary ability to get done what he had decided to do. Compare Reagan with his predecessor, Jimmy Carter, or his successor, George Bush. Carter and Bush were men of considerable intellect, great energy, vigorous attention to detail, and sound personal values. But Carter and Bush achieved very little and were both voted out of office. On the other hand, Reagan was a man of reputedly limited intelligence and education, a medium-quality film actor who told pleasant anecdotes and went to sleep in cabinet meetings (a quality I personally find rather endearing). He displayed no exceptional personal moral zeal or cultural sophistication, and he delegated almost everything. But even his severest critic would not debate that, as much or more than any president in modern times, he was able to implement the program he laid out for himself.

Reagan frequently exhibited a memory as narrow as his smile was wide. But he conquered the inflation, stagnation, and ''malaise'' he inherited, presided over the longest and most vigorous economic boom in America's history, permanently changed the face of American business by largely ignoring antitrust enforcement, fostered an impressive entrepreneurial explosion in which new businesses were created at the rate of about a quarter of a million per year, dramatically shifted the balance of political power from federal to state government, moved the judiciary far toward the right with vast, ongoing consequences, and laid the groundwork for the conservative congressional landslide of 1994.

Perhaps most importantly, Reagan played a key role in taming the Evil Empire, causing the iron curtain to melt and communism to self-destruct.

Reagan engineered this dazzling series of achievements not by omission but by determined, spelled-out-in-advance commission. During the many years of his election campaigns, he told us exactly what he would do if he were elected president. And then, when he was, he did. Anyone evaluating the Reagan years, whether agreeing with his policies or not, must stand in awe of his ability to get what he wanted done. Perhaps more than any American statesmen since Roosevelt—and perhaps more even than FDR—Reagan was willing and able to pursue his clearly defined, far-reaching goals with unrelenting determination. He never deviated from his stated objectives. He never compromised his basic beliefs. He never eased up in his drive to implement them. Indeed, so sure was he of where he was going that he seemed wholly relaxed and easygoing in his approach to getting there.

Achievers who know their goals and aims deeply and fundamentally enough can move forward toward them without the hassle of reexamination, without the struggle of having to revisit their earlier decisions, without having to work hard to keep making what they see as the right decision. They can be tranquil because they continue, without having to second-guess themselves, to *know* what is right.

3

THE CHARACTERISTICS OF THE EXCEPTIONAL INDIVIDUALS

Since there are as many different types of exceptional individuals as there are stories of their achievements, the first questions facing all businesspeople are: How does one recognize them? Do they have visible characteristics in common? How can those traits be identified in advance?

My answer is that, on the surface, achievers differ from each other as much as any group of people can. They come in different styles, ages, educations, nationalities, genders, interests, and attitudes. They behave differently. They reach their goals in different ways. And yet there are similarities. The exceptional individuals of the business world *can* be picked out of a crowd.

HUNGER IS THE KEY

To start, it is obvious that successful businesspeople, and particularly those who are self-made and self-motivated, are typically dynamic, determined, competitive, ambitious, and driven to get things done. Each of these characteristics seems a prerequisite for excellence in business. However, on closer review, I believe that each of these characteristics is, in fact, a facet of a single overriding characteristic I call hunger. Hunger differentiates the overachiever from all others. *Every truly successful person has this characteristic of hunger in huge measure.*

When I first met Estée Lauder—an "ageless" lady but nevertheless "of a certain age"—she was a billionaire and probably the richest self-made woman in the world. But she had lost not one whit of her competitive drive. It was January 1973. Colgate-Palmolive had just purchased Helena Rubinstein, which had been declining but was still one of the world leaders in high-priced beauty products. I had just been made its president, with the assignment of returning the organization to its full former dynamism and glory.

As part of my early self-education in the cosmetics business, I was lunching at Orsini's. The restaurant was then an "in" spot for fashion-industry movers, including Michael Coady, then editor-in-chief now president of Women's Wear Daily *(then and now the industry's daily bible, scandal sheet, and information source). Estée, an impressive woman in a simply gorgeous red suit, made an entrance at the far end of the restaurant. Like an ocean liner, she sailed across the room surrounded by maître d's who bobbed around her like harbour tugs. She berthed on the banquette a mere couple of feet to my left.*

Michael, on my right, leaned over. "Estée, let me introduce Peter Engel," he said, "the new president of Helena Rubinstein."

"Of what?" Estée Lauder demanded loudly, pretending she had never heard of one of her largest competitors, and also making it clear that she was displeased that Michael had even mentioned the matter.

"Come on, Estée," said Michael Coady who could not be intimidated by anyone. "You know perfectly well what Helena Rubinstein is. Peter's their new head."

Estée Lauder stared down her nose at me, examining. Then she extended her finger and stabbed it at my shoulder. ''Some people sell peanuts,'' she said. ''Some sell cashews.'' She paused to make sure I understood. ''I sell the cashews. You stick to the peanuts.'' She turned away, the gospel according to Estée delivered and complete.

I have been a fan of Estée's ever since, a woman who made it from humble beginnings by hard work, drive, and guts.

The daughter of Czech and Hungarian immigrants, Lauder began her long career by personally ''flogging'' beauty creams invented by her uncle. After years of effort learning what women (and department-store buyers) wanted, she broke into the big time in 1953. Her medium was Youth Dew fragrance, a heavy, luxurious, and very expensive fragrance that few women could afford, until they ''discovered'' her well-publicized ''secret.'' It was that Youth Dew bath oil provided the same fragrance as the rest of the line, but at a fraction of the cost.

That ''high price, high value'' concept remained at the heart of Estée Lauder's cosmetics business. For example, she pioneered the idea of gift-with-purchase promotions whereby, rather than lowering the price or indulging in such vulgar antics as couponing or ''one free with one,'' Estée offered ''gifts'' of trial sizes of her products to anyone who bought another Estée Lauder product. Of course what she was doing was exactly the same as giving ''one free with one,'' but offering a ''gift with purchase'' sounded so much more refined!

Estée Lauder's energy was enormous. Throughout her life, she admitted, she never felt comfortable enough to relax. ''If I felt I had made it,'' she explained, ''I would be somewhere nice, like St. Moritz, skiing.''

The most dramatic aspect of this characteristic of hunger universally exhibited by great achievers is that it does not seem to wane. Simply stated, these men and women are *always* seeking to improve things.

I recall Ron Rosenberg, the founder of Dunkin' Donuts, telling me with loud outrage that his son, the president and chief executive officer of the company, had deeply offended him. Apparently, the younger man, quietly proud of his degrees from Harvard Business School and the Cornell Hotel School, and prouder still of the extraordinary growth Dunkin' Donuts had achieved under his stewardship, had objected to his father's continuous needling complaints. ''Aren't you ever satisfied, Dad?'' he had demanded.

''Satisfied?'' the old man yelled at me. ''How could he think I should be satisfied? What does he think? That we've reached perfection?''

The very rich ''are different from you and me,'' wrote F. Scott Fitzgerald. Had he been talking about those members of the very rich who are also self-made, he might have added ''because they are infinitely hungrier.'' These individuals might quickly agree with Cervantes, who observed, ''There's no sauce in the world like hunger.''

For six wonderful years, my good friend, Dr. Jon Goodman, was director of the Entrepreneurial Program of the University of Southern California. She is an energetic, entertaining, immensely intelligent, highly educated, and delightful woman with achievements very few can match. At that time, she had already had a successful business career and she was on the boards of several important companies. Her advice was sought regularly by media organizations, giant corporations, and private entrepreneurs. Her circle of friends was enormous. Her academic credentials were first-rate, and she was a success in every possible respect. I knew no one more capable.

Jon was regularly offered far larger positions in business and academe than the one she held at USC. But for those six years ending in 1995, Jon Goodman preferred fully to savor her good life. Certainly she worked hard and successfully at the USC Entrepreneurial Program, building it into one of the largest and best in the country. But she was so good at her job that she had plenty of time left over to enjoy herself, traveling to Paris or to Bali, or entertaining her friends. She was content with her solid place in the academic and business worlds and did not aspire to the presidency of a major university or company. During that time, Jon was a major achiever—but not, by her own choice, an overachiever.

In the end, however, exceptional individuals of Jon Goodman's class keep achieving. And so, of course, there is a postscript to this story. At the end of the 1994–1995 academic year, Dr. Goodman resigned from the Entrepreneurial Program. She then accepted the task of building EC², an enormous new organization devoted to structuring and implementing new communications techniques and technology in a modern world, under the auspices of the Walter Annenberg School of Communications Management and USC School of Cinema and Television.

Since taking on this entirely new venture, Jon has built a powerhouse. She has built a vast new ''incubator'' for high-tech companies in the communications field, launched a major educational initiative designed to help communications graduates become more successful businesspeople, funded an annual operating budget in the millions, established a two-building facility aggregating 135,000 square feet, retained some of the most advanced technical staff in the world, forged partnerships with most of the leading computer, software, and communications companies in the world, and built EC² into a world leader in its field.

The difference between Estée Lauder, Ron Rosenberg, Jon Goodman, and their ilk and successful people who are not overachievers lies neither in ability nor creativity. The difference isn't in intelligence or judgment. The difference lies in hunger. People who succeed only up to their ability but rarely overachieve (and I shall describe these "facilitators" to action later) are often marvelously genial folk. They do not struggle to effect change. They feel satisfied with the way things are. In contrast, the highest achievers are never satisfied unless they are improving things. In fact, because there is always more left to improve, they are rarely satisfied at all.

SO, IS HUNGER DESIRABLE?

An inevitable question is whether, for these hungry people, their hunger is "a good thing." Are they benefited or harmed? In the case of some of them, such as Estée Lauder, the hunger seems a blessing. For others, the ambition to grow ever bigger leads to immense financial risks.

But obviously, the lack of such hunger is not a problem for many successful and effective but not overachieving businesspeople. They seem to be as happy and content as are the overachievers. The point may not be worth considering in much depth. The fact is, people usually don't have a choice. Either they have an unappeasable hunger to get things done—and then more and more things done—or they do not. D. H. Lawrence wrote that "some men *must* be too spiritual, some *must* be too sensual. Some *must* be too sympathetic, and some *must* be too proud." I, like Lawrence, feel strongly that I have "no desire to say what men *ought* to be." I observe only what is. Sometimes, but rarely (as in the case of Jon Goodman), I have observed that hunger waxes and wanes. More typically, however, at least until old age finally slows them down, the great achievers feel this hunger all the time—and all the time strive to feed it.

All that is certain is that, without this often alogical need for forward motion and the insatiable urge to get ever more things completed, there is no such thing as a true over-achiever. The inner motivation and hunger that drives certain people leaves others alone. Perhaps, in their different ways, both are at peace.

OTHER CHARACTERISTICS OF THE EXCEPTIONAL INDIVIDUALS

Of course there are other characteristics of the exceptional individual: nine main characteristics in all, as detailed below. The issue is how to recognize them. To that end, first we must define precisely what we are looking for.

Psychologists have developed a battery of personality tests that are thought to be useful in helping them understand the personalities of their patients. If these tests worked, then they could be equally useful in helping successful businesspeople recognize the personality of other unusually effective businesspeople. Computerized versions of Rorschach tests might become de rigueur in job interviews.

Unfortunately, personality tests seem to have virtually no predictive value when it comes to differentiating exceptional individuals from run-of-the-mill performers. In spite of all the work done by behavioral scientists in translating diagnostic checks into interviewing techniques, most businesspeople find personality tests useless. This is not to suggest that they do not try them. Many companies use tests. For example, Procter & Gamble has experimented with random questionnaires which they ask successful two-year employees to complete. By averaging the responses, they sought to establish a "norm for Procter & Gamble success." Job applicants were then given the same questionnaire to see how closely they correlated to the norm. The assumption was that the closer the new recruits were to current successful employees across a whole spectrum of abilities and attitudes, the more likely they were to become successful too.

To me this approach seems fundamentally flawed. The norms are set by employees who were hired and who have achieved satisfactory results in the eyes of their bosses over their first two years of employment. No one knows whether that success will continue. And early success probably requires very different abilities than long-term sustained success. More telling, no one knows how successful the people Procter did not hire would become *because* they were outside the norms. They were not hired, but perhaps some went on to great success elsewhere. I do not know whether the company still administers such tests. If they do—and if they asked me—I would urge them not to bother!

Several firms administer more standard psychological tests than Procter & Gamble, but with no better results. And in Europe, handwriting analyses are not uncommon. But for these, and many other "scientific" approaches to identifying the "right" employees, there is no hard evidence that the tests lead to recruitment success. Lacking a control to show how well candidates who "failed" the tests would have performed had they been employed, there can be no test validation. The fact is that candidates who were rejected by one company because of poor test results often do exceedingly well in a different firm, even in a directly competitive one.

While I was an associate professor at the University of

Southern California 1990 to 1995, considerable thought was devoted to the question of how high-potential entrepreneurs could best be recognized and admitted to the Entrepreneurial Program (which was greatly oversubscribed and therefore forced to reject many applicants). Only one objective measure that seems to correlate with future success was found. Grade-point average, GMATS, in-class performance, or any other academic criteria did not seem meaningful. What did count was who applies first. Late applicants seem to lack the drive (the "hunger," in my terms) that true entrepreneurial success demands. At USC, therefore, we accepted the students who have the drive to be first in line when enrollment opened.

At least for the moment, I think it safe to conclude that psychological testing can be ignored as a practical interviewing or job placement tool. Nevertheless, there are ways of recognizing talented potential exceptional individuals. The characteristics of such people can be described with fair accuracy. And, obviously, once they are precisely described, they are far easier to recognize. Let me therefore describe exactly what to look for.

THE NINE ATTRIBUTES OF THE EXCEPTIONAL INDIVIDUAL

There are nine observable attributes that, in combination, make up the true exceptional individual. They are listed here in their order of importance:

Hunger
Intelligence
Energy

Tact
Persuasiveness
Humor
Courage
Optimism
Creativity

Attribute 1: Hunger

The first attribute, hunger, is the most important. While not all hungry people succeed, the psychological traits that can be summarized as hunger are essential to success. Of course, this hunger must be converted to reality. And, to this end, hungry people need a variety of additional characteristics.

Attribute 2: Intelligence

Intelligence is an elusive quality. For one thing, it is difficult to measure. Certainly IQ tests are no sure guide. An organization called Mensa requires that its members have a hefty IQ of more than 140 (an average person has an IQ of 100). Despite their superior intelligence as measured by test scores, many members of Mensa have achieved little.

Most of us know what we mean by intelligence, at least as it is needed in the workaday world of business, even though we cannot clearly define it. As Churchill put it in a different context, "It is like trying to define a rhinoceros: it is difficult enough, but if one is seen, everybody can recognize it." We know, too, that intelligence can mask almost every other weakness, except lack of hunger. Indeed, the opposite sometimes applies: Intelligence can be the antithesis of hunger which it may dilute with too large an influx of logic and common sense.

"Why should I be so hungry?" the intelligent person may ask. "I have all I need."

Since hunger is, after all, an irrational drive, excess intelligence can be a neutralizing force. This, I suspect, was the situation with my friend Jon Goodman during those periods of her life when she felt she had it all and her hunger for achievement abated. Intelligence in business is a very sly asset indeed.

Attribute 3: Energy

Energy, that purely physical force needed to carry out with sufficient vigor the desires created by hunger, is clearly essential to any successful high achiever. Adequate health is generally part of this requirement; an unhealthy person is not likely to be able to generate the energy needed for real achievement. But energy and good health need not entail "wholeness." Franklin Delano Roosevelt, a man barely able to walk, had boundless energy. The greatest British admiral of all time, Horatio Nelson (like C. S. Forester's fictional seagoing hero, Horatio Hornblower) is said to have suffered from severe seasickness every time he set out on a voyage. And, of course, there is Stephen Hawking, among the most influential scientific thinkers of our time. Hawking has succeeded in producing *A Brief History of Time* and, perhaps more significantly, vastly influential and original theoretical work about time and the origin of the universe, in spite of being almost incapacitated by Lou Gehrig's disease. Nevertheless, bad health that lowers the threshold of energy (a heart that can stand no stress or a body racked with debilitating pain) is largely incompatible with great achievement. Just imagine the scale of Hawking's contribution were he not so severely hampered.

Attribute 4: Tact

One of the problems exceptional individuals face when they seek to move people and organizations in new directions is that change, any change, is likely to cause disruption. Thus, the successful achiever must push and push—but not too far. As Jean Cocteau put it, "Tact consists in knowing how far we may go too far."

Another problem that faces high achievers is that they are likely to face envy when their achievements are rewarded. And jealousy among the facilitators becomes a difficult barrier even for exceptional individuals to pierce. As Cardinal de Retz explained in his memoirs in the seventeenth century, "The greatest of all secrets is knowing how to reduce the force of envy."

As a result, it is noticeable that the less tactful, the more abrasive, and the more disruptive achievers are personally, the less likely they are to achieve their ends. It is hard enough to move groups of people imbued with one procedure to adopt another. It may be impossible if the movers are personally disliked and envied. Change is rarely easily or gratefully accepted. Wise businesspeople take care to tread softly when they wield their big sticks. They move mountains not only with vigor, but also with tact.

Attribute 5: Persuasiveness

The ability to persuade (which used to be called salesmanship before political correctness induced us to try salespersonship—which caused us to switch words altogether) is a quality born out of hunger but sired by intelligence. Persuasive people are driven by their hunger to convince others. By virtue of their intelligence, they are able to be persuasive—an ability closely linked to the effective use of words. It is a pretty good rule of thumb that intelligence is closely related to the mastery of language. However, glibness also entails the use of language, and as Willy Loman can attest, glibness alone does not make a good talker into a good persuader.

Attribute 6: Humor

A sense of humor helps release psychological pressure. There is a danger among people of great hunger and ambition that they may drive each other, or themselves, crazy. No doubt, as Shakespeare understood, Cassius's "lean and hungry look" stemmed as much as anything else from the fact that the fellow simply had no sense of humor. Had he had the ability to laugh at life, and perhaps even at Brutus, he might have fared much better. For humor is as valuable in the hungry overachiever as lubrication is to a racing engine. As Arthur Koestler pointed out (not all that humorously), "The luxury reflexes of laughter and weeping emerged as overflow mechanisms for the disposal of at least part of our redundant emotions."

Attribute 7: Courage

Overachievers' lives are replete with risk. They dare to challenge the unknown and the untried, and the unknown is magnified for them because they are driven to explore it to its frightening outer reaches. They are much like explorers striving to discover new lands and new ways to reach those lands. There is risk in new worlds, but the familiarity of oft-trod ground has no allure for them. They need courage to take such risks, knowing that only then can they become what one writer of hyperbole called "butterflies in the skies of commerce."

Involuntary underachievers, in contrast, often have an

immobilizing fear of exposing themselves. Like the servant in Christ's parable who buried the talents entrusted to his care in order to keep them safe, they prefer safety to growth. Thus, they spend their careers in familiar and comfortable surroundings, never daring to visit new lands. As a result, they are quite unable to progress. They remain, literally, landlocked.

It should also be noted that, along with courage, goes intelligence. It is not a brave man who proceeds foolishly. Even the most courageous achievers will tell you that they would never enter a lion's den without checking where the exits are.

Attribute 8: Optimism

Human beings have only a finite amount of courage. It is quickly dissipated if every unknown danger is not only explored fully but also fully felt.

Business optimism is a state of mind that allows people to adjudge risks realistically, but then to feel that things will turn out well. In those terms, Charles Dickens's well-known character Mr. Micawber was no optimist. Although he seemed relentlessly optimistic in the pages of *David Copperfield*, Micawber was but a poor fool who didn't understand the realities before him. His constantly reiterated hope that something would "turn up" was merely a fool's hope. On the other hand, the exceptional individuals' *knowledge* that they are making a decision that has only a 60 percent chance of being correct, tempered with a *feeling* of confidence that it is 100 percent correct, is business optimism of the right order.

Optimism is a necessary attribute because it stretches the finite resource of courage to whatever extent is needed.

Attribute 9: Creativity

The final requirement is creativity. This isn't listed ninth because I hold creativity in low regard, although the truth is that I am less enamored of the fad worship of creativity than many businesspeople and students I meet. Rather, I have observed that first-class people of hunger, intelligence, energy, tact, salesmanship, humor, courage, and optimism can recognize a good and productive idea when they see one. Even if they cannot generate brilliant ideas themselves, they can buy them from others who have talent in that particular area but who are not themselves movers and shakers.

However, I should add that, depending on how creativity is defined, it may turn out to be the single most important of all the nine attributes except hunger. If we define creativity as the ability to develop ideas, I believe it is a desirable but not essential asset. But if we define creativity as the ability to think differently from other people, to solve problems that seem insoluble in order to generate action, then I would agree with historian Arnold Toynbee that creativity is "a matter of life and death for any society."

In his superb book, *The Act of Creation*, Arthur Koestler explains creativity as an act of bisociation that combines two unconnected elements or ideas into one new idea. If you take a detergent and combine it with dirty clothes in a washing machine, you do not have bisociation since you are combining things that are associated by their nature. But if you put detergent into the bowl of water at the base of a cut Christmas tree in order to lower the surface tension of the water and allow more water to be absorbed by the tree, then you have "bisociated" the unrelated detergent and Christmas tree into an idea that will make the tree last longer.

My favorite definition of creativity is: "the ability to find and implement new solutions for the 'impossible.' " The reason I particularly like this definition of creativity is that it links the talent closely to what I call hunger. Social psychologist E. Paul Torrance has written that a creative individual is "fully alive and open to awareness of his own experiences and those of others and seeks to organize them and see meaning in them." Torrance adds that the creative individual has "a need to prove his personal worth and dramatize and display his ideas." He or she may also "enjoy intense, sustained, and vigorous effort to surmount obstacles."

Producing a swarm of quick, facile ideas is often little more than camouflage for inaction. Writers do it all the time, spewing forth concepts and plots for books as a way of avoiding the drudgery of actually writing. Thus, easy answers may gush from underachievers but rarely be observable in overachievers. Some people call this smoke-blowing quality creativity, but true creativity carries with it the determination to ferret out a solution to a problem and the courage to implement that solution.

"Society in general is downright savage toward creative thinkers," Torrance observed. And business is also hard on its driven achievers. Only men and women with plenty of both courage and humor can survive the task of implementing the untried.

Pediatric nurse Sue Benford bisociated when she treated her daughter's stubborn and severe diaper rash with Bag Balm, a veterinary ointment used by farmers on cow udders. When it cured her daughter, Benford developed a new product called Bottom Better, and then built a small but profitable and growing company in Dublin, Ohio, to produce and market it. If ever there were two seemingly unconnected elements, it would be diaper rash and cow udders!

This kind of creativity, where the idea is merely the starting point of implementation, is a rare and necessary talent. The ideas may not be "of the essence," but their implementation is. Just think how successful William Wrigley might have been if his idea for chewing gum had not been innately disgusting! It is those people who have the talent for creative implementation, not just for generating ideas and leaving them unexploited like so many runners stranded on base, who are the exceptional individuals.

These, then, are the main characteristics of the high-achieving personality. But what, you may ask, of that quality renowned by personnel managers the world over, namely "the ability to get along well with people"? Have you omitted it on purpose or by oversight? And what about "team building"?

Of course I agree that these are matters of importance. But I contend that they are the result of other characteristics, not free-standing qualities. For one thing, they are partly a matter of tact, fourth on my list. However, I have known people of great tact but no other achievement attribute, and they could not get along with people at all! They bored even their friends to death! Rather, I suggest that the fact is that tact combined with the ability to create action *is* the ability to "get on with people." This combination is far more important than friendliness or superficial empathy.

Charles Revson, Norton Simon, J. Paul Getty, Howard Hughes, and many others of enormous achievement were not particularly agreeable people. Often they succeeded tactlessly—although they could be more tactful, when necessary, than their remembered portraits suggest. However, even at their most abrasive and least tactful, they were almost worshiped by their business associates. Men like General MacArthur and Alfred P. Sloan, Jr., were cool and standoffish in the workaday world. But their subordinates would have laid down their lives for them. Winston Churchill drove people crazy, but the whole of Great Britain loved him. Whether they are loved or not, most people of solid achievement are admired because they *do* create. Most also end up with large and loyal followings based on the results they achieve. Thus, they are able to "get along well" with their peers and build teams of their followers to a quite remarkable extent.

Many people who experience great personal success have superabundant supplies of charm, especially when it is needed to compensate for those occasions when their drive becomes abrasive. But they incite lasting loyalty not because they can be pleasant when necessary, but because they bring action and movement to organizations and businesses that have been starved for them. People respond to the excitement, to the challenge of action. They become devoted to its initiators.

When a controversial corporate chieftain resigns and half the company "follows the leader" out the door, it is less because of their personal loyalty to that boss than it is a response to the fact that, without the leader's guiding light, life in the organization becomes just plain dull.

Getting on well with people is not a means to achievement; it is a result of achievement.

Now that we have defined the nine characteristics of the exceptional individual, it is time to consider whether and how they can be identified in the short and rather stilted conditions of job interviews.

THE OBSERVABLE PATTERNS

To be specific, two questions arise:

1. Can we guess at the inner qualities of young potential exceptional individuals by assessing their observable outer characteristics?

2. Can all these qualities, and hence the exceptional individuals exhibiting them, be observed and identified during the short and formalized setting of a job interview?

The answers, while not absolute, are generally affirmative.

The most obvious way future achievers can be recognized is by their general passion for living. They simply seem more alive, more awake, more aware. They have read more magazines, scanned more newspapers, talked to more people. They have opinions about everything. They want to learn, to be "in the know." They are as hungry for living as they are for business success.

Stuart Shaw, while a brilliant and successful executive at Procter & Gamble, invented a concept more useful than the IQ rating. Shaw called it AQ, or Awareness Quotient. Rather than measuring intelligence, AQ seeks to determine how wide awake and "with it" people are. Shaw originally developed the concept as a party game, measuring participants' AQs by asking clever, tricky questions drawn from current events. However, in a broader context, high AQs reflect a thorough knowledge of what is happening, an openness to the changing world, and an acceptance of new ideas. This also defines exceptional individuals. It is safe to say that, as a rule, they have the highest of AQs.

Even very young "movers and shakers" work longer hours, waste less time, and assimilate more information—about everything. And that is a pattern that remains with them all their lives. They view less television, unless they happen to be television experts, in which case they view more television and somehow manage to survive without brain damage. They have more interesting friends, more hobbies, more enthusiasms. They "get more out of life." They have the energy and the drive for living, and they burn it freely. Their energy is like love: The more they use, the more remains available. For example, they often travel more than other people.

My friend Phil Beekman was the incredibly determined and hard-working president of Hook-SupeRx. Before that, he was president and chief operating officer of the Seagram Company, and before that, president of Colgate-Palmolive International. Phil's career has been successful by any standards; his wealth is as impressive as his career. But for all that, he rarely relaxed. While he was president of the drug chain, he visited every one of his hundreds of stores several times every year. When you asked the receptionist where Phil was, she would explain that he was at store 72 or en route to store 156. Movement and dedication were a lifelong habit with Phil. When I first knew him, he had just completed two years as the head of Colgate's Latin American and Caribbean business. During his last year in the job, he traveled so much that, including holidays, weekends, and Christmas, he spent only eleven days at home.

But it is not only senior executives like Phil who move so constantly and reflexively. This is a trait that starts early.

One very determined young woman, working for a small Chicago produce-importing company, was able to prove the advantages of travel when, just before New Year's Day, she landed a major contract for her company simply by responding instantly to a blind telephone call from one of the largest fruit-growing companies in Chile.

Wrapped in winter clothes and firmly clutching her briefcase, she ignored the fact that she had been ordered to take New Year's Day off in Chicago. Instead, she arrived to ninety-degree South American weather just before nightfall the next day. Sweating profusely, she greeted her hosts in a few words of halting Spanish she had taught herself on the plane. They found her charming. Her far stronger and less overworked rival, a leading U.S. fruit importer, had also been invited to compete for the business. But they were still writing memoranda and trying to decide whether it was worth paying the expenses of a junior executive's trip. After three days in Chile, now reclothed in local summer wear, the young woman signed a major contract for the fruit-importing business from Chile. There was considerable question as to whether she even had the authority, and she had her fingers soundly rapped by her boss when she returned, shivering without the greatcoat she had forgotten in Chile. But the rap was only for form's sake. The deal was marvelous, a real coup. The Chicago company today is a major winter-season supplier of fruit to much of the country. The woman, no longer young but just as feisty and young at heart, is one of its major players.

I hasten to add that traveling itself is not achievement. There are certain people—international sales executives, consulting engineers, supervising managers, and others—who travel professionally, constantly. They carry passports as fat as dictionaries. Airplanes and hotels are their dwellings, movement their status quo. Among their ranks, in the same proportion as among other groups, are great achievers and minor ones. The *amount* of traveling an executive does provides little clue as to whether he or she is an exceptional individual. The *reason* for the travel can be far more telling.

Exceptional individuals sleep better, when they do sleep, because they sleep from healthy tiredness, not from overweight boredom. They tend to exercise more. There is reasonably consistent evidence that they enjoy above-average health. Certainly, they are rarely obese; overindulgence slows them down, and that is unacceptable.

One important reason for this better health is that high achievers tend to suffer less from the symptoms of stress. Prehistoric humans' metabolism was so arranged that the shock of fear raised blood sugar levels and caused the immediate need to defecate. These were useful physiological reactions; in the face of panic, they provided our early forebears with adrenaline for instant alertness, a "sugar high" for the energy to go with it, and the "lightness" to flee or fight. Since fleeing or fighting both immediately used up the excess sugar and adrenaline, these excesses had no lasting deleterious effect. However, in modern times, our version of panic, that is our worries and stresses, rarely cause us to pick up a club. Rather, we tend to pick up the phone and call our lawyer, which may deplete our bank balance but is more likely to raise our blood sugar than lower it.

Tension and stress, recognized or even unconscious, cause these inborn physiological reactions, but without any compensatory release. No sedate business executive can afford to flee screaming when sales decline. And too few of them are willing to drop what they are doing and rush out for a solid game of squash. On the contrary, in the face of continual pressure and stress, they tend to stay put, working a little harder at their desks to solve their problems. As a result, diencephalic responses build up. The repression of these perfectly natural reactions increases the chances of high blood pressure, diabetes, insomnia, dyspepsia, and even heart attacks.

But the people who make things happen, the exceptional individuals, are pragmatists. They will certainly try harder when things go wrong, but they tend to be less fearful and therefore less likely to be pushed into a flight mode. They are less likely to *feel* like fleeing. While they may feel like fighting, this will simply cause them to "get off their duffs" and go make a few extra sales calls. The physical effort required to do so will help burn off excess sugar. As a result, they are probably less likely to experience the physical symptoms of frustrated flight. Rather, confident of their ability to achieve, they solve their problems, get a good night's sleep, have a hearty breakfast, and get back to their job of making things happen.

THE INCREDIBLE POWER OF THE MIND

The early work of Neal Miller in the 1950s proved that rats can be taught to control their own heart rate. Ramamand Yogi's flabbergasting experiment in 1970 demonstrated, during his six hours in an airtight box, that by will and meditation alone he could live on approximately half the theoretical minimum level of oxygen needed for human survival. Since then, science has been dragged, kicking and screaming, to the recognition that the mind is a powerful medium for controlling even those bodily functions normally considered involuntary. The point is proven, although not yet defined in its particulars, that willpower alone can positively impact health. And as Balzac noted, "There is no such thing as a great talent without great will-power." Talented achievers have the will, and therewith alone they can literally cure themselves of many conditions or even prevent their occurrence.

Obviously, one can exaggerate this observation. It is not true, for example, that depression leads to cancer. However, it may well be true that depression lowers the immune system's vigor, and that can lead to all sorts of unhealthy consequences. Of course, clinical depression, the sort caused by a chemical imbalance, does not spare leaders. But ordinary, reactive depression is less likely to descend upon them. And all depressions are more likely to be fought off, if for no other reason than the fact that achievers are likely to reach for medical help earlier than others. Thus, I believe there is ample empirical evidence to support my own observations that people of great energy and achievement are unusually healthy. In spite of what appear to be tension-filled lives, they are frequently the most relaxed and composed.

Only the problems of drug abuse and alcoholism speak against the general sanity of the overachievers' lives. While statistics are hard to come by (since substance abusers, by the nature of their condition, can't achieve much), my impression is that a high achievement potential is often cut off early by substance abuse problems. Possibly these addictions are greater problems for very action-oriented, tenacious people than for others. The reason, I think, is that the curiosity and courage of these leaders almost inevitably leads them to "try anything once." Of course they have experimented with drugs, the disavowals of most successful politicians (including President Clinton's famous semidisavowal) notwith-standing. Since alcoholism and drug addiction are arguably as much chemical body conditions as, say, diabetes, it follows that "tryers" are more likely to become addicted. And, for that minority of achievers who are prone to the disease, no amount of leadership potential will be a prophylactic. If any-thing, their ability to continue to function for a while as the disease progresses may do them even more harm than if they become incapacitated and "hit bottom" earlier, just as stoi-cally walking on a twisted ankle will simply make it worse. The principal remains intact, however. Except when disabled by substance abuse, doers do.

Thus, the answer to our first question, Can we guess at the inner qualities of young potential achievers by assessing their observable outer characteristics? seems generally affir-mative. There is an excitement and vitality about them that shines through. Even during the job interview, they will be aware, happy to discuss anything the interviewer wants. They will have opinions about almost everything. Their in-terests will range far and wide. They will be relaxed but very wide awake. They will exude health and well-being. Even in their short careers, they will seem to have "done a lot."

However, the larger question remains to be answered, Can all these qualities, and hence the high achievers exhib-iting them, be observed and identified during the short and formalized setting of a job interview? That is what the next chapter will explore.

4

HOW TO IDENTIFY AN EXCEPTIONAL INDIVIDUAL

Identifying and hiring the men and women who are exceptional individuals is the most important thing businesspeople do. It is as true in business as in all worldly matters that people are "the measure of all things." And it follows that only great men and women can achieve greatly. But recognizing the characteristics of an exceptional individual (in current employees or in candidates) remains immensely difficult. Fortunately, now that we have defined their characteristics, we at least know what to look for.

Many people are knowledgeable and competent. They have good track records on paper. When you ask their previous employers about them, you generally receive favorable reports, particularly these days, since giving bad personnel reviews may open the reviewer to legal attack. And of course, during the interview most potential employees seem wide awake and energetic. The question arises, How can we find the real performers, recognize them, persuade them to visit our company for an interview, and then pick them out of the crowd of interviewees?

The first part of the question is relatively easy to answer: You find the people destined to achieve excellence because they are seeking a particular set of circumstances and, being high achievers, they will aggressively search out companies that have those conditions. If you do offer these conditions, they will seek you.

Naturally, publicizing your "face" if you are a small and unknown company may not be easy. However, depending on the circumstances, there are many opportunities for such action. Consider the example of the German retailing tycoon Neckerman.

Shortly after the World War II, a young, very determined German businessman developed the burning ambition to build his small notions retail store into a large chain of department stores. His problem was that no one knew his name. He could not attract customers, suppliers (at least not those who would give him credit), or top-level employees. He had only limited capital.

In Germany at that time there were shortages of almost everything. Thus, the existing big chains—notably Kaufhof, the largest of them—saw no reason to cut prices. They sold whatever they could get at healthy margins. But Young Herr Neckerman knew that situation could not last forever. And he wanted to establish himself in consumers' minds as the low-cost, high-value chain before anyone else started to compete for that honor.

As it happened, Neckerman managed to get ahold of a large shipment of spools of thread. They were in great demand in those days. Because clothes, too, were in short supply, women were constantly repairing and darning their families' old things. The obvious step for Neckerman would have been to sell the shipment in his store. It would have attracted quite a few shoppers and probably built his business a few percentage points.

Instead, hinting that he was desperate for quick cash, he offered the whole shipment to the Kaufhof buyer, and at only a very small profit to himself. The Kaufhof buyer jumped at the opportunity and then he sold out the thread within a few weeks at a solid profit.

It usually takes even an assiduous needle-pusher several months to use up a whole spool of thread. Thus, the whole transaction was forgotten by the Kaufhof people by the time they started to notice crowds of people shopping at Neckerman's. Soon the crowds spilled into the street.

By coincidence, it was the wife of a junior Kaufhof executive who first found out what the fuss was about. As she finished a spool of thread from the lot her husband's company had bought from that nice young Mr. Neckerman, a piece of paper that had been wrapped around the spool under the thread fluttered out. It read:
IF YOU HAD BOUGHT THIS THREAD AT NECKERMAN'S, IT WOULD HAVE LASTED TWICE AS LONG.

Overnight, everyone knew the name Neckerman. From then on, the firm had no trouble attracting the customers, suppliers, and, importantly, the most ambitious of Germany's exceptional individuals as new employees.

Obviously, merely to show the correct "face" is not enough. The face you show must be true, or sooner or later your candidates will sense that your company is not in fact searching for exceptional individuals. Quickly they will decide either never to join or promptly to leave. Moreover, you must be consistent in order to attract the kind of high achievers you seek. Thus, in any advertising, public relations, and especially any word-of-mouth promotion you do—and especially in the first, last, and most emphatic part of the briefing you give to any headhunter you may retain—you should emphasize that, in your company, people are vigorously encouraged to achieve.

Of course, not everyone who applies for your job is likely to be a person of high achievement potential. Many people say they are achievers. Some even think they are achievers. But few are!

Thus, the immediate question here is how to pick the dynamic achiever out of a crowd of "look-alikes" and "wannabes." How do you judge a person's true potential during one or two hours of job interviews? How should you conduct the interview? What sorts of tests should you administer? What should you look for?

Most business owners or personnel managers develop their own interviewing techniques. Some are whimsical. Others are calculating. But above all, the interviewers' techniques must determine whether the applicant has the essential quality of hunger.

An interviewing technique one middle manager loved to use to differentiate the determined from the timid was to say to the applicant, "Sell me something." It often worked, and he continued to use it until one day it backfired dramatically.

"Sell me something," said the manager. Then, noticing a copy of Forbes *lying on his desk, he added, "Sell me a subscription to* Forbes."

The young interviewee made a surprisingly professional sales pitch. The manager was delighted.

"And so would you prefer a three-year subscription or a five-year subscription?" the young man concluded.

"Excellent! Very well presented."

"Well, which is it to be, a three-year or a five-year?"

"Okay, you did a great job."

"Well, thank you. But I have an order form here in my briefcase. It happens that I'm working my way through college selling subscriptions to magazines. I would really like to know if you'd prefer a three-year or a five-year subscription."

The manager was speechless.

"I assume that a man of your caliber would prefer a five-year

subscription. I'd appreciate your signing this order form I'm taking the liberty of preparing for you.''

The middle manager was unable to get rid of the young man, by threats or by laughter, until he had bought a five-year subscription to Forbes! *But along with his subscription, he also knew he'd put his hands on a remarkable young person, a person of real hunger, who was likely to achieve a great deal.*

Eric Morgan, formerly president of British-American Tobacco's cosmetic business, was a brilliant evaluator of interviewees' drives and hungers. Morgan was fond of asking applicants how many uses they could imagine for an ordinary bottle. To think of many uses required an exercise in imagination, of course. But since Morgan typically made the request in an informal, noninterview setting, over lunch, for example, it also gave him a relaxed opportunity to evaluate an applicant's competitive instincts and will to win.

This technique worked well for Morgan but backfired for an acquaintance who sought to copy it. What happened was that the slightly obvious technique annoyed a young man who was not aware that he was to be interviewed, and was not especially pleased at the prospect.

''Well,'' the young man stated, ''that would take me quite a while to list. I'm afraid you'd be bored before I was through and interrupt. That would invalidate my whole approach and upset me.''

''Go ahead,'' the interviewer insisted, thinking he was calling the young man's bluff. ''I promise I won't interrupt.''

''Very well. The technique here is to categorize. First I'll list the uses of the bottle as a container. You could use the bottle to store milk, or beer, or ale, or whiskey, or gin, or . . .''

The young man continued for a full five minutes,

"Then you could use the bottle as a decoration," he changed the subject, "for example, as a lamp to light the hall, or a living room lamp, or . . ."
He continued, listing categories galore, and items beyond counting. If the interviewer sought to interrupt, or even declare himself vanquished, the young man became irate. By the time he pointed out that you could use a bottle as an abstract technique for interviewing, the interviewer swore he would never again use this technique—or interview anyone again without their consent.

Another interviewing technique is to ask sudden, "off-the-wall" questions. An interviewer using this technique might interrupt an applicant's recital of her business background to ask, "If you were stranded on a desert island, what three people would you like to have with you?" The purpose, of course, is to see whether the candidate has the resourcefulness to develop a coherent answer, and the energy, or hunger, to bother. Most people, when so thrown off their stride, are likely to waffle, saying, "I need to think about it" or "I'm not sure."

I once asked my two sons that question. The older boy, pragmatist that he is, answered with a choice of three stalwart and useful people of his acquaintance: one to handle the cooking and exploration of the island, one to build an airplane to escape, and a third to keep the group entertained with his humor. It was a well-considered reply that most of us would support.
But the younger boy, who is nothing if not a creative thinker, instantly had a totally different reply. "I would take a Puerto Rican, a black, and a Chinese," he said.
"Why?" I asked.
"So that we could all start equal," said the ten-year-old.

———

As we discussed earlier, there are no tests of which I am aware that can pinpoint the exceptional individual. To some extent, tasks set to determine interviewees' aggressiveness can help, but they are far from infallible. However, fortunately, there is one rarely used interviewing technique that can differentiate between the extraordinary achiever and the merely successful administrator, if not infallibly, then at least with considerable accuracy.

The technique is simplicity itself. It comes in two parts. The first step is to ask your candidate what he or she views as his or her main strengths. Few people will falsely claim hunger and a drive toward achievement as key strengths if they don't possess them. The thought won't come to their mind. Only people with championship skills will consider mentioning Ping-Pong when asked about special skills. On the other hand, overachievers are very likely to evaluate themselves in terms of achievement because *that is how they think*. Indeed, they tend to be refreshingly frank and precise about all their strengths and in particular, perhaps surprisingly, about their weaknesses.

As a rule, the more achievement oriented people are, the more objective they will be about both their capabilities and their shortcomings. Moreover, they will not want to spend much time discussing their capabilities because they prefer to deal with areas in which they feel they can improve their performances. Even if those shortcomings are few, they will concentrate on overcoming them so that nothing stands in the way of their capacity to achieve. Exceptional individuals measure their own abilities by results—as does the competent interviewer!

The characters in Jean-Paul Sartre's play *No Exit* are underachievers, trapped in a sort of hell because they cannot see or admit their own low level of achievement. But real achievers see themselves clearly. They have a lot to be proud of, and therefore they can feel comfortable discussing where they could still do better. So ask the person you are interviewing about his or her personal traits. You will be delighted at the useful responses the exceptional individual will supply.

The second step, having once established the importance of achievement in the interviewee's value system, is to ask about the specifics of achievements attained. Occasionally, clever interviewees will talk of achievement because they suspect that is what the interviewer wants to hear. But even if they can sound good on the subject, they cannot point to real achievements in their past if they have none.

No technique for pinpointing the exceptional individual is definitive, and more research is needed in this area. So far, neither competent interviews nor the various personality or aptitude tests given by our great companies have proven adequate to the task of pulling out of the crowd those people with outstanding success potential. But actual past achievement, even in high school or in college, is a very sound predictor of future behavior. As Dr. Raoul Sciavi, a professor of psychiatry at Mount Sinai Medical School in New York, puts it, "People define themselves."

Whether exceptional individuals are born, or born and developed, it follows that their inbred drives have been in evidence all their lives. When you ask most people, "What have you done that's out of the ordinary?" they will blankly stare. But occasionally you will find a person who tells you . . . and tells you . . . and tells you!

One of the most dramatic examples was the case of Mike, a meek, fair-haired boy who came shyly into the interviewer's office one day and sat perched on the edge of his chair, knuckles clasped white, and apparently wholly anxiety-ridden.

"What extraordinary experience or idea have you participated in?" *the interviewer started, although she probably felt thoroughly pessimistic.*

Mike shifted uncomfortably. The first syllables out of his mouth were in a high-pitched voice that seemed not quite under control, like that of an adolescent whose voice is breaking. But what he said—and it turned out to be absolutely true—was overwhelming.

"Well, I founded a metal-fabricating plant in a remote village in Mexico, where there was much poverty. Then I sold it to an American firm and came back here to complete my master's degree. And now, you see, I am out looking for a job with a good company like yours." *He paused, and then in a strong voice he added, "A company truly interested in action."* *And he slammed his fist on the table, making the paperweight—and the interviewer!—jump. The young man got the job and went on to great success.*

Another interviewer asked a young man whether he had earned any of his college tuition or expenses.

"Yes I did," *he said.*

"What sort of job did you have?" *The interviewer looked skeptical because the young man was only twenty years old and looked about sixteen.*

"I had several jobs."

"Tell me about that."

"Well, I sold roofs door-to-door," *he stated.*

"Anything else?"

The young man decided to drop his diffidence. "I organized the university typing pool. I published notes for chemistry courses. I translated sales material from German into English in Munich. For an American firm, I looked for sources of tetrafurfurylsalicylic acid in France. I worked as a garage mechanic in England, organized a door-to-door sales force selling mops, chauffeured a limousine from

Toronto to Vancouver, and worked in a cut-rate jewelry store,'' he
said, *and then added cheekily, ''among other things.''*

*The interviewer promptly implied that he was lying, but the
young man had plenty of evidence that he told the truth. The interviewer hustled him out, full of apologies. Later the young man
received a letter, which he still cherishes. It is found on his almost
priceless antique desk, housed in the library of his tasteful and
opulent house, from whence he runs a string of businesses. The letter
said, ''We feel you are somewhat too energetic for the good of this
company.''*

It's not a snap to recognize achievements, particularly if the
interview subjects are young and their achievements limited
by their age. Sometimes it is difficult to put achievements
into perspective because youth makes them seem dispropor-
tionate, sometimes greater, sometimes less great than they
are.

*A businesswoman was sizing up a candidate for a new man-
agement position in her small company. The young woman had
come very highly recommended by a trusted employee, especially
because she had shown such initiative in traveling the globe. But
the businesswoman was not impressed by the candidate. Certainly
the young interviewee had traveled widely, alone, and with considerable savvy and initiative; but she seemed to lack drive and to be
somewhat weak. The travel was the only sign of her initiative. The
business owner decided to probe further.*

''What passport do you carry?'' the business owner asked.

*''I have a British passport and an Italian one,'' the candidate
answered. And then, apparently to make a better impression, she
added, ''My parents came from Chile. Actually, I was born in Canada.''*

The job applicant was no determined traveler. For her, the business owner realized, traveling was the status quo. For this young woman, staying in one place would have been a far more impressive achievement. She was not hired for the job.

I had the experience of interviewing a twenty-seven-year-old man of considerable presence. I immediately liked him, but I could find no outstanding achievements. He had worked for one large company as a salesman and then joined another as district sales manager. Pretty basic stuff. But I sensed something lurked below the surface with this person. He exuded an inner power and energy. But try as I would, I could find no evidence to support my instinctive hunch.

"Are you married?" I asked, trying to steer the conversation in a new direction. Technically, this question may not be legal, but we were just chatting by this time, and I had been describing my family to him.

"Yes." I thought the answer a bit curt.

"Children?"

"Four."

"So many!" I said. "How does your wife manage?"

"Look, is this absolutely essential for this job?" asked the young man. "Frankly, I value the privacy of my home life."

It was a bold, almost rude statement. His chip-on-the-shoulder defensiveness startled me. I was amazed because this quality appeared from nowhere, and he did not seem to be a defensive person. I looked for the reason for his strong reaction.

It took care and a good deal of time, but eventually the story emerged, and the facts added up to an extraordinary achievement. It turned out that the young man's first wife bore twins, and then, tragically, a deaf baby. She had a nervous breakdown and then a full mental collapse. For the early years of his business life, my candidate had not only worked but had also institutionalized his

72

young wife, brought up two healthy babies, and dealt with the tremendous difficulties of raising a deaf son. He had recently found himself a new wife willing to put up with all these difficulties, and together they had had a fourth child. In the context of all these personal problems, his business achievements seemed phenomenal. I hired him, of course, and he became one of the strongest young businessmen I have ever seen, a true overachiever.

Another reason high achievers are sometimes hard to identify is that often they have learned to downplay their achievements and to "internalize credit," as Harlan Cleveland wrote in his book, *The Future Executive*. This may be because, in large companies, "taking credit" is frequently a risky business. Especially if the boss is jealous, it is better to remain silent. Or it may be because, working essentially alone as an expert, say, in computer programming, there simply is no one around to appreciate the achievement. Such "silent" achievers have learned to get the job done but remain relatively anonymous. They leave the kudos to others and keep the achievement as their own inner satisfaction. These people threaten no one, and make no one jealous when they get things done. Machiavelli no doubt achieved more than his prince, Lorenzo the Magnificent, to whom *The Prince* is dedicated. But the achievement was curtailed as soon as, perhaps in spite of himself, Machiavelli started to be credited for that achievement. Lorenzo wanted no partners. Similarly, it may (or may not) have been a certain well-known editor who helped Robert Ludlum become a hugely successful novelist by reorganizing his first drafts into the page-turning best-sellers they are. But Ludlum fired him pretty quickly when the editor had the audacity, and lack of tact, to make that claim publicly. It is rumored that Jeffrey Archer similarly has a "rewrite editor" who whips his works into shape. But, if so, no one is sure, and the editor, presumably, labors on in well-paid, self-satisfied anonymity.

Naturally, it is difficult to identify such modest, "silent" achievers as the real creators of action—and to separate them from those more common individuals who boast loudly of achievements that are not their own. But cataloging the quality of the achievements, and probing for details to differentiate the "doer of the act" from the "teller of the tale" is an effective approach to identifying that key characteristic I call hunger.

As regards the other nine characteristics, they are easier to identify. Indeed, they are so relatively easy to find that I can summarize the characteristic and the technique for identifying it in the following chart—and then need say no more about it.

As anyone studying this chart even cursorily will promptly see, each of the identifying techniques boils down to two steps (which are the same ones described for identifying hunger, variously applied). They are: Ask for the candidate's self-evaluation of the characteristic, and then seek some objective proof that what the candidate says is, indeed, the truth.

Ultimately, there is no complete answer to the question, How do I recognize an exceptional individual in an interview? As Peter Drucker has written, "People-decisions are time-consuming, for the simple reason that the Lord did not create people as 'resources' for organizations." Thus, the essence of the best technique is to give overachievers an opportunity to present a complete picture of themselves. Probe and push to determine what the person has already accom-

CHARACTERISTIC	IDENTIFYING TECHNIQUES
Hunger	As discussed.
Intelligence	a. Ask for a short essay. Judge it less for content, style, or even grammar than for its breadth, its vocabulary, and for any evidence of effort. (The high achiever will struggle to make it as perfect as possible.) b. GPAs and standardized test scores (such as G-MATs, GREs, etc.)
Energy	a. Determine what the candidate *does* . . . the more the better. b. Ask about spare time. High achievers rarely have any.
Tact	This is hard because everyone is tactful in an interview situation. So go back to basics. Ask the candidates whether they are tactful or not. High achievers will tend to think and say no. Probe for examples of limited tact. High achievers will give you examples, but it will generally transpire that they are still getting on fine with the person to whom they were "tactless." Beware of excessive politeness during the interview; exceptional individuals are not sycophants.
Persuasiveness	Candidates who cannot sell themselves to the interviewer lack this characteristic. It's as simple as that!
Humor	This is a desirable but not essential characteristic. Interviewers who have a solid sense of humor will detect its presence or absence in others. Interviewers who do not should excuse themselves and bring in someone who does. Unfortunately, the humorless rarely perceive their own shortcoming.
Courage	This characteristic is not discernable unless the candidate has faced a situation requiring it and can refer to that.
Optimism	I ask one simple question: "Do you think you'll get this job?" Exceptional individuals will say something like "Oh, yes. I think so. And if I don't, I'll get another one that's almost as good." (But for their tact, they would say "quite as good.")

Table Continued

CHARACTERISTIC	IDENTIFYING TECHNIQUES
Creativity	Following my friend Eric Morgan's approach, I keep a picture of a bottle in my drawer. I ask candidates to suggest a dozen unrelated categories of uses for it.*

* The longest list of categories I have been able to devise (on which readers may be able to improve) consists, in approximately descending order of the obvious, of the following:
Container for pourable material (liquids, sand, etc.)
Holder (e.g., for candles, flowers, lamps)
Ornament (e.g., ship in a bottle, vase)
Offensive weapon
Defensive weapon (e.g., broken glass on top of wall)
Container for gases
Toy
Device for heating or cooling (as in "hotwater bottle")
Raw material (e.g., glass for reuse or bottle for reblowing into another shape)
Communication device (e.g. a note in a bottle or an advertising surface)
Symbol (e.g., as corporate logo)
Teaching aid
Interviewing aid

plished. Make sure those accomplishments were real, and not simply a result of following "the path of least resistance."

Business has a tendency to select "well-rounded" people who are competent in all respects and weak in none. This reduces the possibility of hiring a true exceptional individual. Few really strong people lack partially offsetting weaknesses. The activist is often accused of being too pushy. The person driven to get things done is sometimes driven to rage. The individual who is truly creative may, in some respects, be the biggest problem of all. The truly creative person may seem to lack practicality from time to time, or even seriousness. Creative people may seem inappropriately childish on decorous occasions. As the philosopher Eric Hoffer noted, "Both the revolutionary and the creative individual are perpetual juveniles. The revolutionary does not grow up because he cannot grow, while the creative individual cannot grow up because he keeps growing."

Great achievers may, of course, be "well-rounded" too, but they will always distinguish themselves by "pushing the envelope." They will attempt more than ordinary people. Their strengths do not need to be evenly distributed.

Ordinary people with ordinary physiques do not become superstar athletes like Michael Jordan. But "Muggsy" Bogues at only five-foot-three became an NBA star by developing his ball handling skills, strength, and agility. His height is actually an advantage when it comes to pushing the ball up court very quickly. Achievers concentrate on their strengths, understand their weaknesses, and, if they cannot eliminate them, they turn them into advantages instead.

The ultimate question that always faces the interviewer is whether the candidate actually has the strength to do the particular job. President Lincoln was warned that his newly appointed commander-in-chief, General Ulysses Grant, had a drinking problem. "If I knew his brand, I'd send a barrel to all of my generals," Lincoln reportedly replied. The point is that Lincoln knew that Grant, and not McClellan or any of his other generals, was the man to win the Civil War.

If by good judgment or just plain good luck you've landed a person of real achievement potential, of real excellence, it will rapidly become obvious. You may notice that the media department is not only turning out better marketing analyses but is buying media more shrewdly. You may see that new computer programs are being tried and are yielding superior results. You'll observe that sales in your Brazilian subsidiary are booming for the first time. Or that production efficiency in your Grand Rapids plant is suddenly spurting. And if you look farther, and if you aren't dyed in the corporate wool of "We don't work like that," you will find some bright young person working twenty-five hours a day to get things done. You will then know that you were successful in recognizing an exceptional individual. Do not ever let that person go to waste.

5

How to Retain and Encourage Exceptional Individuals

How you accomplish the goals of this chapter's title is straightforward: The most effective way of holding on to any employees is to make their lives more challenging, productive, achievement oriented, and, above all, less boring than they would be otherwise. This need for stimulation, and loathing of its absence, applies particularly to those employees for whom achievement is especially important—and boredom therefore particularly aversive—that is, the highest of achievers.

"The mass of men lead lives of quiet desperation," wrote Thoreau in *Walden*. There seems to be ample proof of this in the sad statistic that the average employed American adult watches forty hours of television per week. Surely, this is a symptom of desperation, because life in front of the television is unproductive, ungenerative, debilitating, and, hence, ultimately boring.

Think about this: On average, we have only about 110 hours available weekly when we are not in bed, getting ready for bed, or getting up. We work (and travel to and from work) some forty-five hours a week. For twelve hours we're out of the house shopping, running errands, mowing the lawn, or eating at McDonald's. That leaves thirteen hours per week when we are home and awake—but not watching television! Of course television is not, in itself, bad, uninformative, or even unentertaining. The problem is that watching TV is essentially a passive activity. It requires no significant level of involvement by its viewers. It washes over people—as do their whole lives—leaving them, like flotsam at the ocean's edge, with little input into their own experience. They rarely experience the joy of making things happen. They can complain, to be sure, but they cannot influence the outcome of their lives. And I suggest that this fundamental impotence over the achievement of their lifetimes is the very definition of Thoreau's desperation.

Of course exceptional individuals do not succumb to this enervating lack of action as much as does the common run of folk. But, unless they are truly overachievers of remarkable capacity, they will be slowed by it nevertheless. One cannot live in a passive, entertainment-dominated society without being seduced into it to a considerable extent. Just as Roman emperors cleverly pacified their populace into placid acceptance of their subservient state by staging gladiator battles at the Forum, so do the high achievers in the television and movie business use all their zeal and ability (and satisfy *their* hunger) by creating TV fare that aims to hook you and me, whether we wish to be attracted or not. Their achievement is our debilitation.

Moreover, a new, somewhat comparable seduction now faces us, and the high achievers among us in particular: The wave of electronic information, especially the Internet, now confronts us. Surfing and searching, chatting and being titillated can take up an amazing amount of our time. And exceptional individuals, being by their nature more curious, investigative, and experiment prone, are likely to be in the vanguard of the explorers. They, along with the rest of us, are at risk of the mental fatty degeneration that accompanies this new sort of time wasting. Fortunately, being the high achievers they are, they are less likely to succumb than the rest of us.

Talk of fatty degeneration brings me to a concomitant observation. It is that a similar phenomenon applies to many areas of our consumption-dominated civilization, for example, food manufacturers, and fast-food chains in particular. They study our tastes with great care, consider our weaknesses, and then create products, and advertising campaigns to popularize them, that we find almost irresistible. Thus, they "force" us to buy and to eat. Struggle as we may, we tend to put on more weight than is good for us. We are part of an overweight society. By effort and willpower, most of us avoid outright obesity. But few of us can avoid adding a few more pounds around our middles than we really need.

I see no conspiracy here. TV executives, Internet suppliers, McDonald's managers, and the many others who seek to have us consume more than is good for us are not out to do us harm. They are not part of a New World Order or a World Zionist conspiracy that plans to destroy our American heritage in a sea of TV, data, saturated fats, or whatever. Rather, they are people of goodwill who sell us those products and services because they believe in what they sell. They strive for constant improvement in their products and services. They measure their success in terms of how much we like them. They are decent people, with high achievers among them, who mean us no harm.

Yet the fact remains that too much TV, a surfeit of information, an excess of fat-laden fast food, coupled with too little challenge and too little achievement, all combine into that quiet despair that Thoreau discerned—and that is, indeed, ubiquitous in our land.

What has this backdrop of "quiet desperation" to do with our ability as employers, interviewers, and managers to attract and hold those people we view as having unusually high achievement potential? It begs us to make their lives at work less boring, more stimulating, more challenging.

There are many ways to improve the quality of the working life of employees. But three fundamental principles inform all these techniques:

1. Challenge employees by assuming they can do more than their apparent credentials would lead one to assume. People are wonderfully resourceful; they can conquer mountains if only they believe they can. And the best way to get them to believe in themselves is for you to believe in them. If their success seems a foregone conclusion in your mind, then it will become one in theirs. The obverse of this, of course, is that if you do not permit your employees the freedom to fail, then you cannot expect them ever to achieve the degree of autonomy and success you want. Thus, the first great law of encouraging achievement is simply this: *Challenge your employees and trust them to meet the challenge.*

2. Establish measurement criteria for achievable goals. If a race had no finish line, no one would ever know whether anyone had won, when the winning took place, or who the winner was. Such a race would be most unsatisfactory. Similarly, any challenge is meaningless if its ultimate goal cannot be measured.

Moreover, even if a race has a clearly established finish line, it would be meaningless if contestants were not told what sort of race it is. Crossing the finish line hours after the winner because you were on foot and didn't know that motorbikes were allowed makes losing feel inevitable and striving to win merely silly. Indeed, winning and losing become largely irrelevant considerations. There can be no feeling of being challenged if the terms of the challenge are not clearly defined.

Yet in business, employees are often given "challenges" that are undefined and/or that cannot be achieved by the employee even in theory. For example, salespeople are often given quotas against which to measure their achievement. But frequently sales results are far more dependent upon forces outside the salesperson's control than upon the individual's selling skills. In that case, the achievement of goals, or the failure to achieve them, becomes a matter of happenstance—and the goals set have little or no influence upon the salespeople's efforts.

In the early 1970s, the Helena Rubinstein company was still a leader in the cosmetics industry. But it was in difficulties. The products were still good but, after years with little innovation, they had become old-fashioned. Little money was being spent on advertising. And the packaging, modified almost whimsically with each new stock unit added to the line, as a whole looked a mess. As a result, consumer offtake was plummeting.

The best salespeople, that is, those who ''sold in'' a full selection of the company's products in sufficient quantities to permit proper display, found themselves in trouble with their customers. When the merchandise didn't move, they obviously could not sell in even more. On the other hand, poor salespeople who hadn't persuaded their buyers to stock the full line faced fewer inventory problems. Moreover, they could blame the slow movement on the retailer's inadequate display. Thus, they had a better chance of continuing to sell.

Consequently, when I took over Helena Rubinstein in 1973, I found that the best salespeople were experiencing the worst performances. And since their incomes were tied to sales levels achieved, the best were earning less than the poorest. Indeed, the salesperson who was paid the highest income when I entered the company had turned in the lowest performance in the prior year.

Naturally, under these circumstances, the better salespeople were quitting to join companies that understood and valued their selling abilities. To resolve the problem, we instituted a unique set of self-measurable, clearly defined, and achievable goals. One in particular was most effective.

It was based on the recognition that the main task for which our sales-people were responsible was to convince cosmetic buyers for stores of the quality of our products. If the buyers were convinced, then they would give our products their best chance by ordering a sufficient variety, authorizing appropriate displays, and pricing fairly. After that, creating consumer *acceptance for the products was outside the salespeople's scope. That was up to our marketing department and our advertising agency. They were charged with finding ways to move the products out of the stores.*

But how to check the salespeople's achievement? It turned out to be simple enough. Most of the cosmetics buyers were women who used cosmetics themselves. Since every cosmetic company provides buyers with any free samples they want, neither price nor availability was a question. Thus, female cosmetics buyers (or the wives of male buyers) used for themselves whatever cosmetics they personally preferred. And so we did "handbag checks." If the cosmetics buyer actually used Helena Rubinstein products, the salesperson received a bonus.

The plan worked. The best salespeople were able to convince buyers of the quality of our products and were rewarded for doing so. Salespeople were rewarded for a task well performed. Buyers who believed in our products did a better job of "pushing" them. And eventually sales to consumers started to rise. Within two years, under this and other business-building initiatives, sales increased almost 50 percent—and the turnover in sales personal dropped precipitously. Once the new program was in place, we rarely lost a salesperson we wanted to keep.

Thus, the second commandment in encouraging achievement is: *Define thy challenges, and make them self-measurable.*

Indeed, this is a theme I shall emphasize several times: Whenever possible, let the assessment made about achievers' performance be their own assessment. They will be harder on themselves than any outside observers would be. And they will take no umbrage from self-criticism, whereas, being human, they may well be offended by—and rebel against—outside criticism that is harsh in any way.

3. Make business life fun. Most people spend the majority of their time working, so the opportunity exists for employers to make this time as stimulating as possible. Simply stated, making work challenging, enjoyable, and *fun* will motivate most employees to devote more of their time to work, or at least, to be more productive. A remarkable achievement, that, but surprisingly easy to arrange since any form of stimulation is "fun" compared to "quiet desperation." Consider the following example of a company with skilled employees, who needed a way to prevent complacency in the office.

Chiat-Day, the iconoclastic advertising agency that pioneered both a new form of advertising and, later, a new form of "virtual office," boasted of the fact that their employees were exploited: overworked and underpaid. Yet they had no trouble attracting the best and the brightest. Moreover, their boast was not idle. For many years—and to some extent to this very day—Chiat did overwork and underpay.

But they made working great fun. The caliber of the creativity, the demands made on everyone, the striving for excellence—all these made the hours of the day fly by. The atmosphere was decidedly lax, with one location eschewing regular offices and simply having couches for their workers. Cellular phones were given out at the start of the day so calls could be made from wherever employees sat on that particular day.

Of course, exploiting your employees is not the answer. Fun can be created in a variety of better ways. Most important is the recognition that work is fun. Obviously, that does not apply if the work is repetitive and innately unchallenging. However, even boring tasks can usually be made less so with a little thought. Perhaps telemarketing, by its nature repetitive, is boring. But if you add the element of competition among teams of telemarketers to the mix, the challenge of winning makes the job far more entertaining. People thrive on competition, especially in groups where losing carries little individual stigma.

There are countless techniques for improving the enjoyment of a job. However, the easiest of all is simply to tell people they are allowed to enjoy themselves working—and then to set that example.

The late 1980s was an exciting time for Mattel. Bob Sansone was turning the once nearly bankrupt company into a money-making machine. Working cleverly and hard, Jill Barratt, his second-in-command, was also tossing her hair and exuding a sort of sexy Sturm und Drang that was quite irresistible. The place was pure fun. I remember one day, as I was waiting outside Bob's office, I heard a secretary on a phone roaring with laughter.

"What was all that about?" I asked as she hung up. "What were you laughing at?"

She thought for a moment. "We're a toy company. We're supposed to laugh," she replied.

The entire toy industry is peopled by the successful Mattel executives of that era. And the far larger company that Mattel is today has its roots in the "fun place to work" it was then. But unless it continues to find ways to create enjoyment for its key employees, it may not remain the giant it has become.

Thus, the third commandment is: *Banish boredom; make life at the office fun.*

Once you have achieved the three basic components of attracting and keeping high achievers—challenging them, letting them assess their own success, and making work fun—the rest of the process is easy enough to implement. It consists, basically, of giving them the tools they need to be successful, and of rewarding them fairly. The tools need be only those that are economically feasible. Achievers have little tolerance for not having an inexpensive computer available when they need one, but they are marvelous at "making do" with hopelessly outdated production facilities because new ones are unaffordable. The remuneration need not be high, or even competitive, provided that it is allowed to rise as the employee's measurable achievement grows. In my experience, exceptional individuals, at any stage of their careers, usually do not mind being underpaid for their work provided future incentives remain real and generous.

Aside from monetary compensation, like all humans, exceptional individuals naturally like to be praised for their achievements. As Boswell heard Dr. Johnson explain, "The applause of a single human is of great consequence." But, as discussed earlier, having learned to "internalize credit," high achievers tend to need less praise than most of us. If necessary, they can accept being publicly underrecognized. Ultimately, though, they usually do mind deeply—and are often deeply offended—to be so privately underrecognized that they feel underrewarded for their achievement. That is an insult that goes too far, and it will cause these action-oriented individuals promptly to move on.

6

EMBRACING CHANGE

Futurist Alvin Toffler coined the expression "future shock" more than twenty years ago, and most of us have been slightly traumatized by it ever since. The world's supply of high technology and specialized knowledge seems to grow exponentially, and this intimidates many people. Indeed, it can be plausibly argued that we stand amidst the first great change in the world's civilization since the industrial revolution, a fundamental change. We are moving from an industrialized society, one that rests on mechanized work, to a knowledge society, one based on computer-assisted information. No wonder we are suffering from future shock. No wonder that, in his 1985 book, *The Adaptive Corporation*, Toffler insisted that a modern manager "must be capable of radical action—willing to think beyond the thinkable." Such significant overriding change can hardly leave us unaffected. And yet, even in the face of such sweeping change, I do not believe that people with the highest achievement potential experience their "shock" as a negative reaction. Probably they are more aware of the changes taking place than are their more passive colleagues. But they do not experience such changes negatively, but with a surge of excited pleasure at all the new ideas abounding. I call such achievers' reactions to the impact of change not "future shock," but "future thrill."

People who yearn for achievement rarely exist without working to make positive change. It is innate in their character that they literally *must* attempt improvement. With their need for improvement and their scorn for the way things are, they keep creating change—which is one reason why so many ordinary people cannot keep up.

Many of us are confused and disoriented by rapid change. Indeed, all but the most amazing of exceptional individuals, those with a real gap in their normal human reactions, are somewhat resistant to change. To paraphrase Abraham Lincoln, change intimidates all of the people some of the time. Moreover, a healthy resistance to change, and to the risk that inevitably accompanies it, is essential to our survival. Too ready an acceptance of change implies a reckless attitude toward risk, and excessive risk takers don't survive, either in evolution or in business. Business executives, even those charged with exploring new opportunities in technology or communications, and energized by that task, nevertheless often prefer to do some things the old way, even if the new ways seem to be an opportunity for improvement. The human race is evolutionarily programmed to exhibit both curiosity (the desire to explore the unknown) and risk aversion (the desire not to leap too quickly into that unknown).

In business, naturally inborn curiosity and zeal for exploration are what make entrepreneurialism—and entrepreneurs—so admired. But it is their equally inborn aversion to the risk of change, the infamous "not invented here syndrome," that lets those same admirable entrepreneurs prosper.

Thus, change occurs fitfully, with even the most adventurous often holding back for a while. But it does occur, and in the end, even "old fogies" learn to accept and ultimately welcome dynamic forward motion. But this takes time. And even the most persuasive innovator cannot—and should not—move a crowd faster than it is willing to move. Trying to do so can be as frustrating as attempting to herd cattle by Lear jet. This is why future young-and-impatient exceptional individuals, when finding themselves unable to move an organization forward quickly, either become obnoxious and are fired, or begin to feel so frustrated that they leave. In a sense, they become the casualties of their own Future Thrill.

OPENNESS TO CREATIVE THOUGHT

One reason certain people achieve so impressively is that they are more open to creative thought, even if they are not more creative themselves. They are willing to "suspend disbelief" and consider new possibilities. Thus, Arthur Koestler, one of the most insightful of all writers on creativity, describes the characteristics of the greatest scientific inventors as "the belittling of logic and deductive reasoning (except for verification after the fact); horror of the one-track mind; distrust of too much consistency." His descriptions apply equally to those businesspeople who get a lot done. They are always keen to consider new options. Moreover, they constantly try new approaches, always seeming to have time for yet one more attempt.

Both in my current business of creating books and in my prior career as a marketing consultant, it has been my repeated task to "pitch" ideas. I can usually tell within a minute of starting my tale whether my listener is open to the new thought. Most are not, and their closed minds are immediately recognizable, in the form of pursed or compressed lips, frowning foreheads, squinting eyes, and, like as not, hands held behind their head as if they needed to protect against the possibility that their heads might be knocked off their shoulders by the impact of a new thought.

The opposite body language is equally obvious. Those open to new thinking will lean toward me as I speak, smile slightly, open their eyes, sometimes part their lips. And they will often nod in agreement as I proceed or sometimes shake their heads, not because they are closed to a new thought, but because they happen to think that my particular new thought is inapplicable or just plain wrong. Closed minds will not dare to shake their heads; they will usually remain still as cobras.

Rarely will the open-minded person "have no time" to see an innovation. For it is an often verified cliché that the busiest of people always seem to have time for yet another project. On the other hand, close-minded executives will keep their doors closed to innovation if they possibly can. They far prefer to discuss with their accountant what has happened in the past than pay attention to some exceptional individual's dream of the future.

SELFISH ALTRUISM

An apparently self-contradictory characteristic of high achievers is that they want to do what they want to do, when they want to do it. But, in a strange inversion of this apparent selfishness, they want to concentrate on doing things that their community needs. The great theater critic Walter Kerr explained that most of us feel compelled "to read for profit, party for contacts, lunch for contracts, bowl for unity, drive for mileage, gamble for charity, go out for the evening for the greater glory of the municipality, and stay home for the weekend to rebuild the house." But the vital achievers and motivators among us do not feel "compelled." If they did, being the activists they are, they might perversely refuse to act. Thus, ironically, their inaction would become the measure of their need to act. As it is, however, they want to do the things that have to be done. Muttering drama critics may be cynically compelled to read for profit, but all over the world a new class of entrepreneurs is loving the task of reading for profit, and profiting even more by changing what they read into an entirely new set of media. There they are, the overachievers, busily reinventing the publishing industry, creating an electronic phenomenon where whole books are just about to be transmitted electronically. All this, before long, will result in a fundamentally new approach to information conveyance. While individually we may resist, collectively we shall eventually live in a world where the clearly old-fashioned, outdated, and inefficient process of writing and reading Gutenberg-style books has been superannuated and replaced by viewing screens or even hearing voices.

INTRAPRENEURING

A great deal has been written about corporate entrepreneurialism or, in the horrible term coined by Pinchot in 1985, "intrapreneurship." As Daniel Jennings writes rather breathlessly, "Large firms . . . have rediscovered the special virtues of . . . harnessing entrepreneurial energy." However, the truth is that very few firms have succeeded. They have paid lip service to the concept of allowing high achievers their heads so that they can develop new businesses untrammeled by the "rules and regs" of the old. But in practice, they have then tried to institutionalize those new achievements. That is, rather than following the advice Peter Drucker meted out in his 1985 book, *Innovation and Entrepreneurship,* in which he advocated organizing to achieve innovation, they have typically bureaucratized innovation to try to turn it into a group process. That cannot work. Innovation by its nature must always be the brain (and love) child, and the implementation responsibility, of a single achiever.

Pinchot emphasized that high-achieving intrapreneurs wish to be involved not only in designing new projects, but above all in implementing them. But he recognized how rarely entrenched middle management, whose only passionate interest is to keep its own job, will allow the intrapreneur to move forward. In a famous warning, Pinchot advised budding intrapreneurial achievers that, if they want to get anything done, they should "come to work every day willing to be fired, to circumvent any order aimed at stopping your dream."

In fact, Pinchot's views are not much different from those of Jean-Baptiste Say, one of the pioneers in the mechanization of the early-nineteenth-century French textile industry and the enunciator of Say's Law. This law states that it is the entrepreneur who drives efficient production by wedding theory to implementation. Specifically, in his 1803 book, *A Treatise on Political Economy,* Say wrote that it is the job of the high-achieving entrepreneur to deal with "an abundance of obstacles to be surmounted, of anxieties to be repressed, of misfortunes to be repaired, and of expedients to be devised." He recognized that "there is always a degree of risk attending such undertakings." He stated that the successful entrepreneur therefore had to possess that "judicious courage which can envisage all manner of risks, and an unperturbable *sang-froid* which permits one to use all means of escaping them." While he recognized that many entrepreneurs, lacking judgment, would fail and lose their money and their reputation, he never seemed to worry that this could happen to him. He was a classic overachiever whose writings, like those of Adam Smith whom he admired, smacked of practical, solid experience. His determination to get things moving is clear throughout his work.

Many researchers have sought to find techniques to foster achievement inside large corporations. R. M. Kanter, in his 1989 book, *When Giants Learn to Dance*, felt that recognition of the achievers was the key. H. L. Angle and A. H. Van de Ven, in their book of the same year (*Research on the Management of Innovation*), described seven "enabling conditions." Van de Ven followed up with an article saying that innovation would only be achieved if top management took on the combined role of being sponsor, mentor, critic, and leader. Jennings and Lumpkin even went so far as to try to throw light on the matter with the technique of MANCOVA (Multivarient Analysis of Covariance). When all the shouting was over, the users of this technique conclude, in Jennings's words, that "innovative organizations are characterized by a participatory management style." *Mirabile dictu*, as my classicist father used to say. Or, in more modern terms, "No kidding!"

The fact is none of these theories hold up (any more than do the more general theories of excellence cited elsewhere). There simply are no absolutes. Research all you will, and what you will inevitably find is that *effective innovation depends on the individual, not on a process, a reward system, or a methodology.* Find the right person, and the innovation will follow.

To describe and decide on the right organizational structure for "the right person" is simplicity itself: Just give 'em what they want!

AND, AGAIN, NECESSITY

We have already examined "necessity" for its role in generating "creative" solutions. In a broader sense, necessity is also the force that drives great achievement. Sometimes it is an inner necessity, purely personally inspired. But even so, for the fuelers of business, that inner necessity is very real. Of course, true (that is, objectively verifiable) necessity inspires massively. Exceptional individuals rise to such absolute challenges with predictable determination. Moreover, such outer necessity may well cause people who are not normally achievers to rise to the occasion. As Albert Camus wrote, "In a time of pestilence . . . there are more things to admire in men than to despise."

Exceptional individuals feel "necessity" even when it does not seem to exist. And whether the "need" is an inner-inspired feeling or an objective outer fact, it remains an enormous incentive to achievement. Moreover, such achievement, in fact, all achievement, becomes the base on which further achievement is built. As Eric Hoffer, the working longshoreman and great American philosopher, put it in *An American Odyssey*, "If, in the end, they [the adventurers and outcasts he was describing] shouldered enormous tasks and accomplished the impossible, it was because they had to . . . and once they tasted the joy of achievement they craved for more." *Craving* may be an operative word. It is the feeling necessity engenders. But it is also addictive; thus, it is also the feeling engendered by prior achievement. In business, it may well be true that people who crave, achieve—and those who feel no craving don't.

Necessity is not only the mother of invention. It is the father of achievement!

If you doubt the importance of necessity in creating action, consider the amazing surge of necessary and creative business activity now taking place behind what used to be called the iron curtain, where millions of people survived under a mindlessly rigid system of central government.

I visited East Germany only a few days after the Berlin Wall collapsed. In Weimar, famous as the hometown of Goethe and, of course, as the birthplace of the Weimar Republic, I met the son of one of my father's former associates. The son was a strong, determined fellow of about fifty who had grown up under the communists. For many years, he had run Weimar's best bookstore in a wonderful location right on the Goetheplatz, the very center of the city's commercial life and, now again, tourist life.

"What will happen to your position once the State no longer controls your bookstore?" I asked.

"I shall buy it for myself," he stated proudly.

Aware that private capital was hard to find in the former East Germany, I wondered aloud, "How will you find investors willing to leave you in charge, and leave you with a fair ownership share?"

"Easy," he boasted. "I shall borrow the money to buy the store from a bank."

His bookstore did not seem like a bankable deal to me. He didn't own the building. He needed more operating capital than would be covered by his inventory. And he seemed to have no other collateral. Still, perhaps he knew something I didn't. And maybe I could help. "Do you have any other collateral than the store itself?" I asked doubtfully.

"Oh, yes," he assured me proudly. *"I shall use my guaranteed State income as bookstore manager as collateral for the bank loan."*

Compare that to the new, necessity-driven breed of post-communist entrepreneurs now dominating the scene throughout the former Eastern bloc countries. Not only are they now fending for themselves, but they are leading one of the greatest social and commercial experiments in history, having created thousands of private enterprises to replace the creaky, inefficient, omnipresent state monopolies of the past. Men and women formerly ignorant of the workings of capitalism and taught to hate even its basic precepts have created a whole business infrastructure from scratch. From the earliest, post–Cold War barter exchanges of Russia to the revitalized shipyards of Gdansk, there is a new "Wild East" of entrepreneurship. Fine artists who were supported by the State now run commercial art galleries; armaments factories are producing machine tools. Retail stores are advertising, fast-food chains have sprouted everywhere, and former apparatchiks have become rich in commerce. Indeed, it should come as no surprise that so many of the successful new entrepreneurs were also successful in the communist hierarchy. Even there, some people had the capacity to achieve and thus rose to positions of relative authority (albeit little actual achievement). As free enterprise replaced communism, the achievement potential of many of these people flowered into impressive actual achievement.

Of course, at the same time, inflation is rampant, crooks and mafioso dominate whole sections of industry, people are disgruntled with high prices, politics is a shambles, and one or several new revolutions are entirely possible. But no one ever said that the achievement of an entrepreneurial democracy was easy!

"The success of radical institutions . . . is ultimately dependent on whether they can become institutionalized," Daniel Jennings wrote, quoting a view expressed frequently by R. A. Burgelman in the mid-1980s. The Russian situation shows just how wrong this view is. Goodness knows, communism was institutionalized enough. Today's post-communist Russian world will survive or fail depending on how many exceptional individuals it spawns, how much of their new freedom and power they can hold, and how little they become institutionalized.

Necessity turns many people into aggressive and effective doers. We are evolutionarily programmed to survive, and it is an evolutionary inevitability that we should meet real necessity with real achievement. That is why we so often observe a great leader emerging "coincidentally," just at the moment when a crisis of necessity requires one. It is surely no coincidence that Winston Churchill, largely ignored before the crisis of World War II, was given almost dictatorial power during that conflict. Nor is it surprising that, as soon as the crisis was past, the people of England voted him out of power, replacing him with the small, rabbit-faced Clement Attlee who epitomized administrative competence and the comfortable solace of "smallness." Similarly, albeit on a lesser scale, it should be no surprise when a dynamic leader replaces the prior "bureaucrat" in a foundering business— often at the very last moment, only just before all is lost.

But if our evolutionary heritage requires us to fight for survival when disaster looms, then it must also teach us to sit back and relax when things are going well and there is little need to strive. With no challenge, most people feel little need for great achievement. It is no surprise that, with the outbreak of peace after the World War II, America elected the shrewdly placid, golf-playing, and easygoing "Ike" Eisenhower as its two-term president. Thus, it is only those rare people who feel an inner challenge all the time, even when others feel none, who become the all-the-time movers of mountains.

Unfortunately, not every crisis brings a rescuer. Great companies, like Electronic Data Systems, Microsoft, or Wal-Mart, are built by extraordinarily effective entrepreneurs. Not infrequently, these companies flounder when their creator dies and no one as good emerges to take their originator's role. The jury is out on those companies. But where is the Borgward automobile company, which, in its heyday under the genius mechanic Borgward, created some of the most exciting engineering breakthroughs in the early decades of the automobile? What happened to Gimbel's or Loft's candy or the Packard? Has anyone heard of Gestetner copying machines lately? Or of Osborne or Kay-Pro computers? What are the chances for Wang? Under its founder, An Wang, it dominated early "word-processing." Now it languishes, perhaps to recover under a new leader, perhaps to fade away gradually under the "leadership" of facilitators with no achiever to guide them.

Myriad firms that made decent, sometimes excellent, products at fair prices in their time no longer exist. Most should have survived. But they didn't because no determined achiever felt that their survival was necessary. Without such a person to keep them healthy, they slowly declined and decayed. Eventually, they went out of business or into various forms of reorganization and subjugation. At best, some of these companies continue to eke out a limited existence. They wait, perhaps in vain, for some new human dynamo to *feel* their need—and thus to feel driven to take over their helms and steer them back to glory.

While hundreds of railroads succumbed, a few metamorphosed into successful and growing industrial corporations. Most traditional candy companies disappeared, but Mars and Hershey remain impressively profitable. The Sears catalog, the famous "Wish Book," became an unfulfillable dream and had to be terminated. But now a thousand other direct-mail catalogues, including some from Sears, collectively fulfill our every wish, and do so profitably because they are largely run by individuals who cause them to be so very precisely focused. A hundred automobile companies ceased to exist or, like American Motors, were swallowed up by their rivals. But Ford thrives, Chrysler, after flirting with death, is doing well, and General Motors has, at long last, rebounded.

The many failures and, happily, at least as many successes prove that, with the right leaders, most companies in most industries can succeed. Unfortunately, no guarantee exists that such people, the ones with that strange surplus of drive for achievement that lets them sweep past all obstacles, will be found in time.

Obviously, if change is traumatic for most people—indeed for all but the most extreme and effective of exceptional individuals—then to maximize the achievement an organization can make, every effort should be made to "detraumatize" change.

Successful achievers do this in four main ways:

1. Make change itself the status quo. Sometimes it is possible to change "the way we do things" so that it doesn't really feel like change at all. Thus, companies involved in high fashion or fad industries recognize that need to relaunch themselves constantly, sometimes several times each year. Obviously, a fashion company that knows that each spring and fall it has to bring out a completely new line of clothes will not reject the "change" involved in doing this. However, in most businesses, change is not a requirement. Nevertheless, by careful planning, the concept of constant change can sometimes be built into the corporate culture.

3M Corporation has built new-product development and the theory that goes with it into its corporate culture. Throughout the organization, everyone works mightily to develop the attitude that anyone can create a new product—and that everyone should. Thus, not launching new projects (the absence of change) becomes traumatic because it violates the status quo.

2. Make "change" synonymous with "improvement." Even when a company is not, strictly speaking, in the business of change, it can so position itself as to seem to be, both to outside observers and to its own employees. Thus, "high-tech" companies often make a point of trying to invalidate all existing technology just about as soon as it is created. As a matter of policy, they start developing a new, often dramatically improved product as a matter of course virtually the day they bring out the prior product (itself also a major improvement over what came before). In this way, the negative concept of "change" is converted to the positive one of "improvement."

3. Set the goal of change in advance of the change itself. Microsoft is notorious for announcing new software months, and sometimes years, in advance of delivery. Obviously, part of their strategy is to "hold open" the opportunity so that it is not killed by competition before Microsoft's version of the product becomes available. However, another very important effect of this approach is that it accustoms people to the upcoming change well in advance, so that, when the change finally comes, it has the advantages of real novelty and improvement, without the disadvantages of newness. It already feels "old hat" and therefore carries with it few of the disadvantages of the trauma of change.

4. Place exceptional individuals in charge of change. As with all things in business, ultimately the only truly satisfactory

way of effecting change in an organization without causing debilitating fear and resistance is to place the job of making that
change into the hands of some high-achieving individual who is
more upset by keeping things the way they are than by changing,
and improving, them.

The questions we shall now revisit in greater depth are:
Just where does this need for action spring from? Why do
some people have this huge need to achieve? And how do
you tell who those people are?

7

THE EXCEPTIONAL
INDIVIDUAL'S DRIVE TO
ACTION

A great deal of theoretical work has been done by psychologists who seek to measure the "need to achieve" or the "motive for success," in other words, the cause for the hunger that lies at the heart of all achievement potential. But the practical question is, Are these discernible characteristics of high achievers' qualities you can develop in yourself and then begin to incorporate into your own business career? To answer this question, we must first dig more deeply into the genesis of hunger.

The most fundamental explanation of the hunger for high achievement stems from the universal drive for dominance that is observable in humans as well as in a thousand other animal species. In almost every society of insects, birds, reptiles, and mammals, we ordinarily see a clear and important ranking, a well-established pecking order. In *African Genesis*, the anthropologist Robert Ardrey wrote: "Every organized animal society has a system of dominance. Whether it be a school of fish or a flock of birds, or a herd of grazing wildebeest, there exists within that society some kind of status order in which individuals are ranked. It is an order founded on fear." Although Ardrey's book was published in the

1970s, I am aware of no research contradicting this basic principle.

In every society, individuals instinctively know those whom they must fear, and those to whom they must defer. They also know those who must defer to them. An awareness of rank must have appeared early in the evolutionary process, and evidently remains with us today. I am frequently amused to see the degree of awe, some might call it terror, truly powerful people inspire even in those over whom they hold no actual sway.

In the days when, as a senior executive, I inhabited a huge corporate office replete with plush furniture, acres of windows, and its own executive washroom, quite a few of the employees entering my office would literally shake with anxiety. But so would visitors who did not work for me but who felt themselves to be my juniors. (Visitors who themselves inhabited comparable offices were, of course, unaffected by mine.) Then, as the wheel turns, one day I was back on my own, making more money, as it happens, but without any visible trappings of power. Salesmen who had roared with nervous laughter at my jokes only months beforehand now barely smiled. Twenty-five-year-old office boys now wandered into my office saying "Hi, Pete." They were not crowing about my changed circumstances; they did not know what the real difference was. They simply felt differently in my presence. I am convinced that quite often their new feeling of camaraderie and "reduced awe" was instinctive, simply a gut reaction to my reduced degree of apparent dominance.

Zoologist Jane Goodall spent many years observing chimpanzees in their African habitat. Her observations strongly suggest that dominance is the result of achievement. She suggests that chimpanzees develop dominance by learning that they *can* achieve. Initially, hunger drives them. Later, the experience of achievement itself leads them and their peers to assume that they *are* dominant.

The same principle seems to apply to humans: Over-achievers are those who are so certain of their own superior abilities and strengths that, right or wrong, their self-confidence convinces their peers. Being accepted as leaders, they can then achieve more than their actual superiority warrants thus justifying their feeling of dominance. It is an upward spiral.

My friend Benton James (name changed) was a pretty successful middle manager in Procter & Gamble's brand management hierarchy. But he was not slated for vast success. However, in some ways he positively shone: He looked the part of a senior executive from the top of his conservatively groomed, thick, dark but gray-sideburned hair, to his perfectly polished wingtip oxfords. His voice was strong and assured, his manners were impeccable, and his golf handicap was low enough to be impressive but not so low as to indicate time stolen from work. His wife was a Daughter of the American Revolution. His kids called me Sir. His dog fetched the paper and sat when ordered. Benton was a man's man, a proud alumnus of Yale and the Marines, and an equally proud member of the Cincinnati Country Club, the NRA, and Skull and Bones.

Yes, Benton was loyal, decent, God-fearing—and smart enough to leave Procter & Gamble before his mediocrity became obvious. He took a job as executive vice president of a medium-sized toiletries marketer, with a contract that he would be CEO within a year.

He failed and they fired him, buying him out of his contract.

After a few weeks of playing golf with the right people, Benton became president of a Fortune 500 consumer goods company, with a five-year contract and an impressive joining bonus. They gave him a heavy indemnity in lieu of his contract when they fired him eighteen months later.

Benton played some more golf and became chairman of a large marketing consulting company. At last he had found his metier. Clients loved his solid values and sincere manner. The advice he gave was sound, too: it was generated by the firm's very bright, albeit not as personable, juniors.

Unfortunately, the consultancy purchased an operating consumer-goods company and put Benton in charge. They retired him two years later with a pension for life!

Does their habit of achievement convince dominant individuals of their own strengths? Or do they merely *feel* superior and thus achieve: a self-fulfilling prophesy? Like so many intellectual conundrums, this one seems to demand an answer but is as difficult to resolve as whether the egg preceded the chicken or vice versa.

By a giant leap of conviction, admittedly no more than hinted at by the observations of anthropologists, I suggest that achievement *creates* dominance in human beings. It is an almost circular argument: Achievement creates a feeling of dominance and that feeling fosters achievement. Quite possibly, the original ability to achieve greatly is inborn, or at least inculcated at a very early age. But everyone has some ability to achieve, and that latent talent is likely to be enhanced by all the achievement that is gained. So the argument is linear, optimistic, and repetitive: People with any ability to achieve become ever more effective as they create achievement. As every "old wife" knows, success breeds success.

Nevertheless, matters are never simple when we consider human behavior. For we can demonstrate that, even though the potential for dominance may be an inborn trait, it can remain merely latent until the right tools come along.

Jane Goodall describes the ultimate emergence to dominance of a certain middle-ranking ape. He was large of heart but rather puny of body, and therefore unable to win his battle of bluff against his huge competitors however great his determination. His salvation came in the form of two empty gas canisters he found lying around Goodall's camp. Grabbing them, he rushed at his dominant ape leader, banging the cans together to make a fearful clangor, howling as he went. The noise was too much for his giant antagonist, who cringed and retired. The smaller ape, never letting his canisters far out of his sight, overcame his inadequate size and realized his inborn ambition for dominance. As time went on, he remained dominant, having to resort to using the canisters less and less frequently.

In the tiny office I inhabited after I left the reflected status of a senior position in a Fortune 100 corporation, I had no metaphysical canisters to rattle. I was back to being a middle-of-the-road business ape! But one day the late Phil Dougherty of *The New York Times* wrote a laudatory piece about my new venture. Suddenly I was back in power, my clangor heard, my jokes funny again, office boys subservient!

Thus, bolstered by observation and experience, I maintain that although the potential for achievement—and hence dominance—may not be inborn, it is undoubtedly determined early in life. Even among animals, dominance isn't mere physical superiority; much is a matter of voice and bluff, not tooth and claw. While the dominant male in a chimpanzee society is unlikely to be the weakest, he need not be the strongest. But the top chimp must be viewed, by others *and by himself,* as being the most powerful.

Although the talent for "dominance based on achievement" cannot be created from whole cloth, it can be nurtured where it exists. A psychological multiplier effect exists. People with the ability to achieve can have that talent enhanced enormously by allowing them to make significant achievements early on. The confidence that these first faltering steps bring may be sufficient to loose a torrent of achievement. There is an upward spiral: Achievement leads to the confidence that allows achievers to perform to their utmost limits—and perhaps well beyond their apparent ability. So clever managers initially give new employees some task to perform at which they are mostly likely to succeed, and, in providing such a positive environment, boost their employees' egos, help them build actual achievement, and thus greatly enhance their potential for future achievement.

But beware! For there is a pernicious tendency toward "smallness" lurking here. It is encapsulated as clearly as anywhere, in Karl Weick's Theory of Small Wins.

SMALL WINS AND LARGE

"The fastest way to trigger an IRS audit is to exceed the 'normal' range on one of your deductions," explains the ad for Turbo Tax, "America's #1 Tax Software." The implication, widely accepted by taxpayers and tax advisers alike, is that being audited by the IRS is innately undesirable. One should not put oneself in the way of an audit, so goes the popular wisdom. Thus, you should not exceed the "normal" range of deductions, even if you feel legally justified in doing so and could save quite a lot of money. In other words, when it comes to taxes, you should not "push the envelope." Of course, this means that you will probably pay more taxes than necessary. To avoid the *risk* of being audited and having to pay back taxes, you are actually accepting the *certainty* of paying those taxes now. Swapping a certainty for a risk seems pretty silly on the face of it. Moreover, in the case of the tax situation, the advice is even worse than that. For almost all tax cases are settled by compromise. Thus, what is really being swapped is the certainty of making a full payment against the risk of having to make a partial one. Only tax advisers who want no extra work and do not much care that their clients pay extra tax would make such irresponsible "don't push the envelope" recommendations.

"Bulls make money. Bears make money. Pigs lose!" This is an adage popular on Wall Street. It means, simply, that you should be satisfied with the small gain. If you hold out for the "killing," you may lose your stake. It is far better to make a small gain and live to invest another day. In other words, when it comes to investing, you are well advised to make consensus investments and never "push the envelope." Of course this is not the advice of Warren Buffet who made several billion dollars pushing the envelope to its utter extreme. Rather, this advice comes from the mouths of countless hand-wringing investment advisers and stockbrokers, all carefully contained within their white-picket-fence mentalities.

Karl Weick is one of the most influential proponents of the "small wins" theory. Writing in the *American Psychologist* in 1984, he advocated that, this theory holds that managers should challenge their staffs only with small tasks, ones they can easily achieve. That way, no one gets "stressed out." He has remained true to that view. For example, as recently as 1993, he wrote in a major magazine, *Dividend*, that "highly aroused people [by which he means people under stress] find it difficult to learn a novel response, to brainstorm, to concentrate." Weick makes it clear that he does not mean that managers should break down big tasks into small pieces. "Small wins seldom combine into a neat, linear sequence with each step being a demonstrable step closer to some pre-determined goal," he insists. Rather, he believes that humans become so traumatized by large goals that they cannot perform adequately. Small goals lead to small wins, which make their achievers more self-confident—and likely to achieve even more small wins. It is a seductive idea that ties in neatly with my view that achievement fosters more achievement.

But, of course, this amounts to extending the view that "success breeds success" ad absurdum. Indeed, following Weick leads to the clear and present danger that mediocrity is about to be elevated to a new level of positive business theory. Lou Gerstner, soon after taking the reins of IBM, announced that "the last thing this company needs right now is a vision." And not long ago, *Fortune* magazine ran an article extolling the virtues of managers who, rather than paint some vast picture of a greater tomorrow, concentrate on doing everything well today, on just running things, on being "on top of things." "Just-in-time" inventory management tries to make your production facilities so flexible that you neither run out of goods nor are forced to build inventories. Just-in-time inventory management and the theory of small wins seem similar: Fix problems and take advantage of opportunities only as they arise. Don't create a dream about the future. Don't follow some grand strategy. Whatever you do, keep your head down. If you take care of today, without excess, without long-term ambition, without a dream, why then the future will take care of itself.

Weick goes farther and suggests that "the massive scale on which social problems are concerned precludes innovative action because bounded rationality is exceeded and dysfunctional levels of arousal are induced.'' In other words, even in setting national policy, in planning for the health and welfare of our descendants, in working toward integration, in seeking a solution to world hunger, we should not view the goal, only the immediate, limited, achievable steps.

More and more business schools are teaching Weick's theory; more and more managers are accepting its principles (even if they have not heard of Weick); more and more politicians are hiding behind its comforts; and more and more thinkers are embarrassed to take time off to dream.

With all of them, I beg to differ.

After twelve years as a schoolteacher, and dissatisfied with her impact (and probably her earnings), Jan Davidson, then in her early thirties, founded a nonprofit tutoring center and decided to improve its performance by writing educational software to drill students in math and vocabulary. By 1994, Davidson & Associates has annual sales of $60 million and a market value of $290 million. But Ms. Davidson has not, apparently, learned her lesson. She is still leapfrogging ''small wins'' and concentrating on big ones. As Newsweek described it in February 1994, she is ''working tirelessly as an education activist. She coaxes business to give more to education, goads competitors to build more educational value into their products, and prods teachers to push for change.''

Perhaps Ms. Davidson will eventually go out of business, sell out to a larger, more ''efficient'' organization, or lose her vision and become an administrator. Perhaps after a while a ''small wins'' successor will stop reaching for the stars and reach for a 5 percent annual growth rate instead. But whatever happens, Ms. Davidson, and her husband, who assists her, will know that they made a *huge* difference to the way kids learn, how much they learn—and thus to how much they will contribute in the future.

Watching a pride of lions hunt is immensely exciting. In silent cooperation, they form a semicircle downwind from their prey and edge forward imperceptibly. The gazelle looks up, sensing something amiss. The lions freeze, four of them, crouched lower than the waving grass, brown fur blending into brown soil. The gazelle, still aquiver but relaxing slightly, lowers her head to eat another morsel. The lions inch forward.

Suddenly, marvelously coordinated, the two lionesses at the edge of the semicircle spring forward. But they do not aim directly at the gazelle; rather they bound straight ahead, parallel to their target's logical escape route. The gazelle hesitates, wondering whether to flee in the opposite direction.

Like well-trained receivers in football, the charging lions turn inward, starting to cut behind the gazelle. She could still make it if she went flat-out; a gazelle can easily outrun even the fastest lion. But just as she is about to take to her heels, the remaining two lionesses, still crouching and invisible, spring at her. The gazelle succumbs to utter panic. Lions are tearing toward her from four corners. Desperately, she leaps off in one direction, only to change direction with her second bound, wasting more time and sealing her fate. The lions are on top of her, snarling and bloodthirsty. In seconds, it's over.

Gradually, with great dignity, the male lion, who has observed but has not participated as his females hunted, moves toward the kill. He eats with deliberate contentment, while the females, hunger and blood-lust straining their faces, wait. If one comes too close, the master snarls briefly to remind her of her manners. When he is done, the females eat their fill. Finally, the cubs come trotting up together and gobble the remains.

At last, replete, the lions leave the carcass for the hyenas and walk heavily to a sunny and comfortable nearby meadow.

I cannot imagine a more impressive win. But it is a classic "small win." It leads nowhere. Tomorrow, when they are hungry again, they must hunt again. Perhaps they will out-maneuver another gazelle. Perhaps they will not be as lucky and be forced to share a jackrabbit. Quite possibly, they will exhaust themselves and go hungry. In lean years, many lions die. And even when game is plentiful, a lion's life, filled though it is with small wins, is tough and risky.

Lions are *not* the kings of the jungle; humans are. That is because only humans can see beyond their immediate need, to a greater goal. Lions can cooperate in a hunt in very so-phisticated ways. And they have far greater power and speed than any mere human. But they cannot strive on some "mas-sive scale." For example, they cannot dream of a lion society where gazelles are easily available and no lion dies of star-vation. They cannot think beyond the immediate problem of personally getting enough to eat today. They cannot push the envelope at all.

Undoubtedly, in many ways, Professor Weick is right. If you are intent only on gaining that next promotion, stick to the rules, learn and implement your company's "procedure book." Next quarter's profit, your semiannual sales quota, a good grade on your next performance review—all require that you conform. If you do, you will suffer no blame. If you don't, you are taking a risk.

Ah, but if you do take that risk, you just might, to some tiny but still just perceptible degree, move the whole world forward. And, with the confidence that such a victory brings, you might well implement another achievement large enough to leave its trail. And another. Now these are what I call real "small wins."

THE NECESSITY OF SELF-RELIANCE

A second and different view of achievement lies in American philosopher Ralph Waldo Emerson's thought that the way "to do is to be." The person who achieves "exists in a crowd for himself and lives the way he thinks, not caring how others think of him."

Emerson's essay on self-reliance is one of the most illuminating writings on how to be—and by inference how to foster—a high achiever. It demonstrates that the ability to get things moving forward need not be based on extraordinary talent, but rather can result from an extraordinary desire to develop and state your own clear beliefs, and then convert them into action.

"To believe your own thought, to believe that what is true for you in your private heart is true for all men—that is genius," Emerson wrote. "In every work of genius we recognize our own rejected thoughts; they come back to us with a certain alienated majesty." It is this "recognition of self," really a mixture of self-esteem and consequent self-reliance, that is a vital part of the ability to achieve great things.

This combined characteristic (at the risk of oversimplification, let us call it self-confidence) includes the need, even the duty, to accept responsibility. Exceptional individuals do not have to be dragged and pushed into the committee to rebuild the church roof. They volunteer. They are not merely willing to accept responsibility. Rather, they value it and actively seek it. Once having volunteered, they then listen carefully, synthesize solutions to the problems being discussed, and surprise all the others by telling them what to do. Chances are, they will later be in the vanguard of those actually doing it.

To repeat the point, it is the "doing of it" that fosters future achievement. The message is very basic: Get the job done, and each successive time a job looms, getting it done becomes easier. Before long, by the very doing of deeds, you too can gain the confidence Emerson described, the confidence of the high achiever, the *over*achiever.

I am amazed by how difficult it is for most people to make decisions. Frequently, business trains its executives so well to see alternatives—and to recognize the danger of choosing the wrong one—that instead of teaching effective decision-making, it inadvertently inhibits the executive's ability to make any decisions at all. At USC, many of the graduate students I taught seemed almost pathologically unable to choose one single path from the myriad alternatives open to them. "The owner should seriously consider four alternatives," their essays would start. They never could decide on only one.

"Start your essays with the words, 'This recommends . . . ' " I would cajole. "That way you will force yourself to be decisive."

But about a third of my students appeared congenitally unable to comply.

The problem of indecision gets worse for men and women as they move farther up the corporate ladder, for the negative results that stem from making the wrong decisions become graver. Occasionally, this causes a kind of temporary paralysis.

I once worked for the chief executive officer of a $250 million European company whose indecisiveness became so severe that one day he became unable to decide which of several clients to visit first. To force him to action, I had to give him an itinerary, which (I untruthfully claimed) had been set up to accommodate the clients' wishes. "You have no choice," I insisted. But he was no fool, and he must have guessed I was lying. So it was an agonizing moment for both of us, the more so because this was a man whose intellect and grasp of alternatives I had long admired. He had simply reached the point where he was assailed by too many alternatives.

The ability to make decisions without agony and to accept easily the responsibility for them, right or wrong, is one of the defining characteristics of anyone destined to achieve. These people are existentialists; they view their contribution as valuable only to the extent that it is tangible. They never confuse thought with action. Either they make what they have thought about actually happen, or else those thoughts have little importance to them. They recognize an obvious truth: A "difficult" decision, that is, one where two alternatives seem almost too close to call, is actually the easiest decision of all. While others agonize over which is the best decision, exceptional individuals flip a coin and merrily follow its direction. They know that whichever way they go, they have just as good a chance of being right!

In general, the people who get things done are great pragmatists. They are more aware than others of their own strengths and weaknesses, and they accept such self-recognition easily. Nietzsche's Zarathustra was "afraid of my own thoughts and afterthoughts," but for achieving businesspeople, not superhuman at all, the acknowledgment of "the heaviest and blackest" in themselves is not over-

Yves Rocher was a quiet, shy, completely introverted man who grew up in a village in northern France. Yet he founded a highly successful French cosmetics concern under his name. When I met Monsieur Rocher, he had just had stomach surgery and could barely walk. He greeted me bent deeply at the waist and clutching his stomach. He was painfully shy, spoke no English, and was under no obligation to see me for what he knew was at best a ''long shot'' opportunity. But see me he did. Quiet and introverted he was, but for all that, utterly determined to achieve action if there was even the remotest chance of it.

I would guess that there are as many quiet successes as there are noisy ones. Nevertheless, extroversion is frequently thought to be synonymous with action. I believe the reason is that the ebullient person frequently appears to be very open—open to ideas, solutions, attempts. On the other hand, there are certain types of quietness that probably are incompatible with an open mind: the personality types that are closed of mouth because they are closed of heart. But I doubt whether there is much evidence in the psychologists' journals of any correlation between an open mouth and an open mind. The extrovert may be appearing to agree, may be promising to act. But action, when it is actually measured, depends not on who talks about it the most, but on who *does* the most. Gertrude Stein wrote that "a rose is a rose is a rose is a rose" (thereby excluding all extraneous coincidence about flower gardens, assistant groundsmen, and so forth). Paraphrasing, I suggest that they act who act who act who act! Certainly if quietness is not a symptom of a closed mind, then it need not be a symptom of any inability to achieve.

In practical terms, then, we should closely observe

achievers in business rather than just listen to those whose talk encourages our attention.

THE STUFFY PROFESSOR SYNDROME

This myth, that action is inhibited by thought is nonsense on the very face of it. If it were true, all human endeavor would be disastrous indeed, for all action would be essentially thoughtless. Only a cynic of really overwhelming bitterness would believe that. On the contrary, most of us would agree that thought is a vital precursor to action and, with John Locke, we would feel that "the actions of men [are] the best interpreters of their thoughts."

Warren Buffet and Bernard Baruch, for example, perhaps the two most successful investors Wall Street has ever known, both explained that they occasionally took several days off just to think before taking a decisive action. From time to time they had to insulate themselves and give themselves time to think in order to prepare for their carefully considered action.

Sometimes wisdom appears to be the opposite of action simply because the wise do not rush to action precipitously, but take time to think. Sometimes, of course, speed is desirable, and then the wise will move "faster than a speeding bullet." Stevenson, Roberts, and Grousbeck make this point very clearly when they write, "Prestart analysis must have a very strong mandate in favor of decisiveness, timeliness, and go or no-go actions. You cannot get bogged down in analysis paralysis."

The fact is that there is nothing in the least antithetical between thought and action.

THE BUSY BEAVER SYNDROME

The important thing to understand in the context of this myth is that, appearances to the contrary notwithstanding, "activity" is not the same thing as "action." The former involves effort without results; the latter involves results regardless of effort. Indeed, as Dr. Johnson wrote, "There is no kind of idleness by which we are so easily seduced as that which dignifies itself by the appearance of business."

"Events are not rushing anywhere, we are merely consuming them at indigestible speed," Russell Baker wrote in one of his delightful columns in *The New York Times*. He and Dr. Johnson are both right: Frequently, frenetic obsessive activity is a large stumbling block in the way of getting anything done.

Having now exploded the three most pernicious anti-action myths—namely that action-oriented people have to be noisy about it, that thought is antithetical to action, and that busyness is action's symptom—we can proceed to discuss the specifics of "the anatomy of action."

THE ANATOMY OF ACTION

There are, to be precise, six discrete steps to action. Let me summarize them first, and then expand on them in the balance of this chapter. The six steps to action are:

1. Find the blockage. Whatever is standing in the way of action. There must be such a problem, otherwise the action would

long since have been taken. That's just how achievers are. However, beware! The blockage is rarely what people initially think it is.

2. Communicate. Once you understand what the blockage *really* is, share that information with the people involved. Explain clearly the genesis of the blockage. Since the problem is rarely understood, its causes are almost never recognized. If they were, there would probably be no blockage.

3. Develop a solution (or, occasionally, admit that there is none, and write off the action as impractical). The reason solutions are often hard to envisage is usually because people don't really understand the problem and its genesis. Once these factors are known, an on-paper solution is often surprisingly simple.

   Where a simple solution does not present itself, a creative one must be sought. Later in this book, I shall digress briefly to illuminate the subject of business creativity and how it can be taught, nurtured, and then positively exploited.

4. Make people *want* to solve the problem (or at least do this for the exceptional individuals you are trying to encourage). This is a matter of motivation. And the most important motivator of all is to give people the tools and guidelines to monitor their own performance. As I have emphasized before, it is infinitely better for *you* to conclude that your performance needs improvement than for me to tell you so.

5. Foster stubbornness. We shall *not* accept no for an answer. Our back is against the wall; we *have* to succeed. Thus, as Stevenson, Roberts, and Grousbeck put it, "the purpose of analysis is not to find fault with new ventures or find reason for abandoning them. Analysis should be considered as an exercise in what to do next more than what not to do."

Interestingly, this "encouragement of stubbornness" or tenacity, is not contradictory with Step 3, where the conclusion
may indeed be that the problem is insoluble. Stubbornness
should not be equated with stupidity (although it often is). A
project may be "doable" or not. Stubbornness is valid when
the project is theoretically feasible and the achiever fights un-
relentingly to make it work in practice. Stubbornness becomes
stupidity when the project is infeasible, or when its achievement is so difficult that the achievement is not worth the trouble. Pyrrhus achieved his goal, but his only real achievement
was to leave us his name as the adjective that means "not
worth the price of the achievement."

6. Honor success. People need to be both honored and rewarded for the success they achieve. Of the two, being
honored is by far the more important. You will find that,
when people demand a higher reward, it is usually because
the "rewarding" has been allowed to become synonymous
with the "honoring."

Those, then, are the six principles of action. Let me now
explore how they should be implemented in practice.

Step 1: Find the Blockage

The first step, underlining my view that thought is the necessary precursor to any successful action, is to do the thinking
necessary to define the problem. There is probably more time
and effort wasted in the business world on administering
events without defining problems than on anything else.

"Our sales are declining. If this continues, we'll go
broke," wrote the slightly hysterical CEO of a medium-sized
toy company. No one disagreed. I was called in because I was
experienced at building sales. But it took only a few days for
me to realize that the root of the problem was not that sales

were plummeting; that was the painful symptom of the problem, not its cause.

The actual reason for the declining sales was that, in an industry where innovation was all, my clients had few really new products. There was no excitement; consumers generally felt that the company's products were good but dull. They were uninterested in buying. Detailed market research indicated that consumers answered the question, Why don't you buy the company's products? with one of several versions of the same basic answer: What have they done for me lately?

Further investigation showed that the lack of new products was still not the core of the problem, only a more clearly defined symptom. The reason for the lack was that, even though a number of competent people in Research and Development were making a considerable effort, senior management could never agree as to which new product should have priority. This constant disagreement resulted in a "stop and start" situation. In the end, nothing much got done. Even the good developers had lost heart; few new products were finalized, and they were generally the least controversial ones. And, of course, "least controversial" meant the least innovative, the least exciting, the least *new*.

At this point in the analysis of the problem, it appeared that the constant disagreement among the middle-management executives was close to the "heart of the problem." But why couldn't they agree? Almost immediately, the answer became clear. I attended a new products meeting, with the president presiding. He was the eldest son of a very successful father who had founded the business. When Dad died, Junior took on the job, apparently to his own surprise. He had the training but not the guts for the position. Within minutes of the start of the meeting, it was clear he would never decide which new product or products should have priority. Without his lead, the company was bound to flounder. There was nothing I could do; reluctantly I resigned my commission.

Before long, the company had declined so far that its bankers forced the replacement of the owner's son with a new chief executive officer. This man evidently analyzed the "problem" even faster than I had. Then, simply, quietly, he designated which items were to be the top-priority, new-development products. Within months they were on the market and the company's sales started to climb again. "He's some salesman," they said. They were wrong. "He is a man of action!" they said too. And in that they were right.

Step 2: Understand and Communicate the Problem

The method of chasing down the symptoms until the heart of the problem is discovered boils down to asking and then re-asking the simple question "Why?" It is necessary to continue to ask that question until it is simplified right down to one clearly defined and easily understood problem, a problem so simple that action can immediately be implemented to eliminate it. This technique, which I call "The Repetitive Why," can be readily practiced. Here is an example of its use:

a. A company's sales were growing faster than the industry average, but profits were declining. Generally in the industry, there were substantial economies of scale so that the rising sales should have led to rising profits. (As noted above, a general problem is almost always a symptom, not itself the problem.)
Why?

b. The answer was that the company's cost of goods, as a percentage of sales, was rising, whereas, by rights, it should have been falling. (Had this been taken to be the problem, management would have commanded, "Lower the cost of goods!" But no one would have known how, and therefore no action would have resulted.)

Why?

c. Analysis showed that the reason for the cost of goods increasing was that raw material prices were rising in line with inflation but selling prices were climbing more slowly; nor were selling prices mounting as fast as competitive prices. (No wonder sales were up: Prices were unrealistically low. The obvious and necessary action was to raise prices. To be on the safe side, however, it is always worth asking "Why?" one time more than "necessary.")

Why?

d. Because the sales department's bonuses were tied only to very ambitious sales increases, regardless of profitability. Naturally, therefore, salespeople tended to cut prices (or sell "bargain" merchandise) in order to build sales, even if that hurt profits. To do otherwise would be right for the company but would mean less sales growth—and therefore less income for the salespeople.

At last the heart of the problem had been uncovered. In considering the solution, it was clear that the sales personnel should be rewarded not just for growth, but rather for *profitable* growth, and that growth targets should be set at far more realistic levels. When this plan was implemented, unit sales growth did indeed slow because average prices rose, but, for the same reason, dollar sales growth actually accelerated, and profits started to climb.

Sometimes a problem traced back to its source by the use of "The Repetitive Why" will identify two wholly different core problems as understood by two competent managers who each hold a different perspective. In summary form, here is an example of "The Repetitive Why" used in such a situation.

The symptom being probed was that deliveries of a pharmaceutical company were frequently short shipped because the wrong inventory was on hand. This problem existed even though there were no raw material shortages, strikes, lack of factory capacity, or other obvious reasons for the shortages. In this case, "The Repetitive Why" technique was used with both the factory manager and the sales manager.

As an illustration of how such different viewpoints can color understanding, their answers, presented here in tabular form, looked like this:

Sales Manager:	Factory Manager:
a. The problem is slow deliveries and too many back orders.	a. The problem is slow deliveries and too many back orders.
Why?	*Why?*
b. Shortage of inventory. They never have enough products in stock. Why don't they just produce enough?	b. Long inventories but the sales forecasts are always wrong so we have the wrong inventory on hand.
Why?	*Why?*
c. The factory production schedules are based on incorrect forecasts.	c. Sales always sells the wrong merchandise.
Why?	*Why?*
d. Their historical data is wrong, and they won't listen to us tell them what we're going to sell.	d. Because of a fundamental lack of discipline in the sales department.

Sales Manager:	Factory Manager:
Why?	*Why?*
e. Because their historical data of what we sold is based on the previous data, which was also wrong because we couldn't sell what we didn't have.	e. That's just the way salespeople are. ("They need a new sales manager. I could show them a thing or two.")
Proposed Solution:	**Proposed Solution:**
Have Sales do the forecasts. Then we'd always have available what we sold.	Fire the sales manager and have the factory manager control the sales department. Then they'd sell the stuff we make.

Naturally, both "solutions" were invalid. But now the problem was clear: inadequate forecasting because of bad communications between Sales and Manufacturing. A practical solution was promptly implemented by an enlightened CEO. He had the chief financial officer work closely with both Sales and Manufacturing to develop the best possible sales forecasts and manufacturing schedules. Within a few months, the system was working nicely, the sales manager and the factory manager actually became friends—and the problem was resolved.

The first principle of action is to understand the problem.

As clearly shown by the above example, once the problem is traced back to its root and clearly understood, it has to be very carefully explained to everyone involved by the manager in charge or, if the problem is sufficiently widespread, by the president of the company.

The second principle of action is to explain what is going on and why.

Step 3: Develop a Solution

Often the solution becomes obvious the moment the problem is understood. Dozens of books have been written about problem-solving as if it were the main activity of business. But it is not. Usually, solving a problem is one of the simpler parts of the anatomy of action. Only on fairly rare occasions is it intellectually difficult to solve the problem once you have defined it completely and explained it clearly.

Theodore Levitt of the Harvard Business School emphasized that the question of "what our business should be" is a vitally important part of the solution to business problems. He believed, presumably, that this is a very difficult question to answer. I think otherwise. Indeed, while the question must be answered, the answer generally lies in choosing what the exceptional individual "believes in." The railroad's answer to Ted Levitt's question: What should our company be? amounted to "We don't know." That was clearly wrong. But they could have chosen from many alternatives. For example, had they chosen to emphasize transportation of the individual, they might have started producing automobiles. Had they defined their role as "speedy transportation of crowds of people," they would have become airlines. Or had they clearly stated that their business was freight, they would have stayed with trains, but added trucks, freighters, and containering to their business. None of these definitions or the resulting actions would have been wrong. Each could have been equally well justified by statistical analysis. After all, the airline, automobile, and freight industries have all thrived (occasional problems in each notwithstanding). Thus, any one of these definitions, the latter one of which they eventually gravitated toward, would have saved the railroads a great deal of financial hardship.

Nevertheless finding a solution is not always as easy to do as it is to say. Even though solutions to most problems are available, finding them sometimes takes creativity. In order the understand the application of creativity to the business world, it is necessary to define the difference between innovation and invention. Of course, both are based on creativity. The difference between them is that, since the effectiveness of business institutions can be evaluated by the amount of their achievement (in dollars, brownie points, or however achievement is measured), a change in methodology designed to improve the amount of the achievement is an innovation.

Conversely, invention is not necessarily related to achievement. While an invention may solve a problem, it is just as likely to give rise to new ones. Leonardo da Vinci, and much later the Wright Brothers, did not invent the plane in order to solve a problem. They invented it merely to invent it. Certainly, the plane eventually solved a variety of transportation problems. But it also gave rise to huge new problems, ranging from air disasters and bankrupt airlines to losing one's baggage at O'Hare during rush hour. One might define the difference between innovation and invention by explaining that innovation is needed in order to keep the baggage under some degree of control and thus increase airport efficiency, while invention involves the creation of a new type of homing device designed to track birds that may eventually be transformed (by innovation) into a new way to track errant suitcases.

Thus, the third step to action is find a good solution—

even if none seems initially obvious. It need not be the "best" solution, just a simple, clear one that leads to progress.

Step 4: Motivation

Most problems, while easily solved in theory, are a lot more difficult to solve in practice because their solutions require the combined efforts of many people, most of whom are not high achievers and would much prefer to be left alone. Thus, this fourth step, getting people motivated to act, may well be the most important part of the anatomy of action. *Nothing happens if people don't want to make it happen.*

Elsewhere in this book, I have described the overall aspects of motivation and tried to define some of the differences between the ordinary and the overachieving businessperson. Here, therefore, I would like simply to summarize some of the specific leadership techniques that are worth applying in instances where the solution to a problem is well understood in theory, but vigorous action is required to implement that solution in practice.

There are four techniques of motivation that are more important than all the others. They are as follows.

a. Understanding and Feedback. One of the most dramatic facts about human communication is that it is often ambiguous and ineffective. Time without number, two people believe that they have accurately understood what each has said only to discover later that they completely misunderstand. Sometimes two people can negotiate and sign a whole written agreement and nevertheless a fundamental disagreement persists. Henry Kissinger engineered a written agreement between North Vietnam and the United States to settle the Vietnam War. As a result, the Americans did what they wanted and withdrew their troops, understanding that thereby the war would end. The

North Vietnamese did what they wanted and conquered the South. Yet apparently both sides acted according to their understanding of the agreement. And Kissinger won the Nobel Prize for peace.

In the business world, to make sure that every understanding is as complete as possible, especially if the agreement is a casual, everyday one, it is usually helpful to use the technique of "feedback." Let me give you an example:

Statement of sales manager to salesman: "I think it might be a good idea if you raised your number of calls per day. At the moment you're averaging ten. Would you please see if you can make it eleven?"

Feedback A: "I'll certainly consider that. And I'll let you know what part of my in-store activity I'll have to cut out to make the time."

Feedback B: "I have considered that. I believe it would be impossible."

Feedback C: "Yes, sir. I will call on eleven stores per day from now on."

In the first case, the salesman thought he was being asked for an honest evaluation of whether he could increase his calls. In the second instance, he felt the manager was asking his opinion, not issuing a directive. In the third case, the salesmen decided that he was being give an order.

(Of course, each of the types of feedback above may be incomplete. For example, the salesperson in Feedback C may not be adding "and I'll also go and look for another job.")

Generally speaking, such feedback is enormously helpful because the first communicator can find out immediately whether his or her message has been received the way he or she meant it. In the above example, the sales manager could easily have told either of the first two respondents that they misunderstood, and that what he meant was that they should make eleven calls. Alternatively, had he not meant that, he could have said to the third respondent, "Wait a second; before you increase your number of calls, I would like to know what you'd have to give up."

I warn, however, that "hidden feedback" is also important. Since it is unspoken, it must be observed by the empathetic manager from body language, the lack or presence of eye contact, and dozens of other subliminal signs.

b. Make the job fun. High achievers are typically followed in business situations, sometimes with almost slavish devotion, because it is fun to participate in action. Or, as Ogden Nash put it:

> *No, you never get any fun*
> *out of the things you haven't done.*

I suspect that working at, say, Microsoft is rarely dull. Since humans are easily bored but hate the feeling, people unable to overcome boredom without help will follow far the leader who can.

c. Have the forthrightness—and often the courage—to tell people where they stand. For most of us it is heart-wrenching to tell employees (perhaps ones who have become friends) that they are performing inadequately. But it is even harder to have to fire them. And that is what is likely to happen if inadequate performance is allowed to persist. Thus, it seems to me that one vital job of the motivating "boss" is to tell employees honestly where they stand all the time. Shortcomings should be dealt with immediately. For the only way to engender a feeling of true job security is to make sure no one is ever surprised by being fired or demoted. This takes a combination of honesty and fairness. Where a company habitually demotes or fires people without telling them well in advance where they stand, then all those employed can never be sure that they themselves are safe. And few people will dare to create action if they feel unsafe. Why stick your neck out to make things happen if you fear that the first time something goes wrong you will be out of work? We all realize that the risk of something going visibly wrong in the short run is higher where there is constant striving for action than where the status quo is acceptable. But not taking that risk, that is, allowing inaction to breed, is almost always fundamentally wrong in the long run.

   d. "Bruce's Spider Syndrome." Robert the Bruce, you may recall, gathered the courage to make yet one more attempt to fight the English by watching a spider fall repeatedly from the ceiling and then climb stubbornly back up its thread. Eventually the spider made it. In the short run, so did Robert the Bruce. This motivator is simply perseverance. If you refuse to give up, if you will brook no thought of quitting or losing, if you remain undeviatingly convinced of eventually reaching your *achievable* goal, then so will those you lead toward it. As Churchill put it: "Never give in. Never, never, never—in nothing great or small, large or petty—never give in except to convictions of honor and good sense."

   Of course, persistence is a trait that exceptional individuals bring to the corporate table themselves. What we're discussing here, remember, is "hidden feedback." By showing persistence, one can often lead others to share the same quality.

   The fourth principle of action is *communicate to motivate*.

Step 5. Tenacity

We have already touched on this as one of the four great motivators. But tenacity is so important that it bears repeating here. (This writer is nothing if not tenacious in making his point!)

   In this context, it is essential to both foster stubbornness (i.e., tenacity) and to avoid its excess (i.e., mulishness). The "good" tenacity means simply an unwillingness to admit to impossibilities, the persistence to continue in the face of adversity. We are all taught from the womb to recognize the stringent limitations of our difficult world. How can a baby, vainly struggling against its swaddling clothes, be other than frustrated and convinced of its limitations? How can that baby, after being symbiotic with its mother for months, suddenly be left screaming, immobile, and alone for an interminable twenty minutes, without being convinced of the impossibility of most things? How can schoolchildren, unable to grasp calculus and facing the idiotic question "What don't you understand?," learn more thoroughly of their own frailty? Yet we ask the adult, grown from the constantly frustrated baby and schoolchild, to be open to the idea that any achievement is possible. For most of us that concept is not only intuitively improbable, it is downright wrong. Only the highest achievers are able to ignore their own limitations. Better yet, they are often able to convince others that there are no insuperable limitations anywhere in view.

Of course, as noted above, some things *are* impossible. Not accepting that fact becomes, at some point, not a laudable act of determination, but one of lamentable stubbornness. The problem is that the borderline between the two remains blurred. Many things, from electricity to space flight, which were certainly "impossible" in their time, have become commonplace.

How, then, can anyone make the decision of what is possible and what is not? Can we defy gravity and learn to float upwards without mechanical support? That is impossible—until someone invents a way to make it possible. And yet, as a practical matter, a business based on the possibility of developing an anti-gravity device would probably not be worth pursuing. Thus, canny achievers really never believe that something is impossible. There is no room for that concept in their thinking and feeling. Instead, they ponder whether a particular task is "worth it." The anti-gravity device may be possible ultimately—at least if the acheiver wants it strongly enough and works toward it hard enough—but as a practical matter, the project may not seem worthwhile.

The key here is that such judgments have to be left to the exceptional individuals to make for themselves. It is their intuition that counts. It is their ability to overcome or to ignore the perception of their own limitations which differentiates exceptional individuals more clearly than any other quality.

Thus, the fifth principle of action is *stick to it long after it seems impossible, right up to the point when it really is impossible.*

Step 6. Reward Achievement

Of course, everyone agrees in theory that high achievement should be highly rewarded. But, in practice, that principle is often ignored. Worse, it is frequently violated.

The CEO of a large public consumer goods company had acquired a highly profitable, but much smaller, multi-level marketing firm. The day after the acquisition, a large, noisy, aggressive woman wearing an enormous hat broke past the two secretaries guarding the office of the CEO of the parent company and breezed into his office.

"Hiya, Pete," she said, dumping herself into his chair. "How're you doing?"

The elderly, conservative CEO, never before in his life referred to as "Pete" ("Peter" by his peers, and "Sir" by everyone else) was disconcerted and annoyed.

"I would prefer it if you would make an appointment," he said acerbically.

"Hell, Pete," she grinned at him. "Why would I do that? I'm one of your major shareholders." She paused. "Anyhow," she added with a smirk, "the last time I looked, I earn more than you do!"

The subsidiary's commission structure was changed only days later. No longer could the subordinate expect to out-earn her boss. It took her only a few weeks to quit, taking a full quarter of the subsidiary's saleswomen with her. The sub's sales dropped; its profits plummeted. It was years before the business recovered to its former level.

Obviously, this should be a cautionary tale to any businessperson: financial reward should be in line with financial achievement to whatever extent that can be measured. In this case, the executive foolishly chose to punish a personal breach in etiquette at the expense of his company's profits.

But, in most cases, the specific contribution of any executive, even an overachieving one, cannot be measured specifically. Thus, while outstanding achievement should be rewarded, sometimes that reward cannot be in direct proportion to an employee's actual performance—and, for practical reasons, it may still have to fall within certain remuneration guidelines in order not to throw off the employer's entire salary schedule.

Unfortunately, this means that truly exceptional individuals sometimes simply cannot be paid all they deserve. Fortunately, however, this is generally not necessary to keep them fully loyal and motivated. What is needed instead is a plan whereby their superior contribution is recognized by management—*and widely broadcast to their peers.*

The symbols of superior performance, the plaque on the wall, a free trip given as a prize, an invitation to the Board of Director's luncheon, the right to fly on the company plane—these mean more to overachievers than pure money. Indeed, in many ways, money is more important as a means of recognizing exceptional service than for its inherent value.

So, the sixth principle to action is *honor the achiever—and do so as publicly as possible.*

9

THE EXCEPTIONAL INDIVIDUAL'S SUPPORT SYSTEM

Within the great teeming beehive of commerce, exceptional individuals cannot achieve personal excellence without help. They need the support of people around them who are willing and able to help them implement their dreams. Such implementors are far more common than real achievers, but they are still rare enough to be valuable. Thus, they should be cultivated, encouraged, stroked, and rewarded. They are the "arms and legs" the achievers need to reach their goal. And they are clearly different in kind from that vast array of drones who not only do not achieve, but who, sometimes unconsciously and sometimes on purpose, impede progress.

Supporting the small cadre of high-achieving personalities, there is a much larger group, lower on the ladder of achievement but still on the same continuum, who are the workers who make great achievement possible. In the right circumstances, and given the right encouragement, some of these implementors can move up the ladder of effectiveness and become achievers in their own right.

Whether one considers the annals of war or the stories of maroonings survived, it is a frequently recurring theme that great danger or hardship inflicted upon a group of rather ordinary people often brings forth one member of the group who, by courage, imagination, a willingness to accept responsibility, and the ambition to conquer the challenges facing the group becomes its leader. Almost gleefully, it seems, the new leader takes on the seemingly impossible task of confronting and surmounting the obstacles the group faces. When the danger is past, one of two reactions occur. Either the hero of the moment returns to being an ordinary implementor whose achiever skills remain unchallenged and therefore unutilized, or such individuals, empowered by the experience, gain the self-confidence and credibility to continue their high-achieving lives.

In the ordinary pursuit of business, this same principle pertains: Challenging the group of employees—creating a feeling of "necessity"—is both an effective way of pulling forth the maximum level of achievement of which they are capable and an excellent way of differentiating between the implementors, those who support achievement, from the drones, those who tend to hold it back. These tasks can be made progressively more challenging, instilling a sense of confidence in earlier projects and separating the "wheat from the chaff" in later ones.

FACILITATORS ARE THE ALLIES OF ACHIEVEMENT

Many people achieve a valuable kind of "low excellence" in business. These are the facilitators. While they may not be able to create or restart a business on their own, facilitators have great value in that they can maintain and sometimes accelerate the growth of an already-moving company. They are effective in the furtherance and even the acceleration of "the way we do things." They even generate sensible innovations to improve the efficiency of "what we do." And they are quite capable of making small and important adjustments to keep a preexisting initiative on course once they understand what that course is. Thus, all things considered, these men and women are essential to the overachiever in creating action.

Facilitators are typically easy to spot in any organization since they are fundamentally and directionally different from employees who work reluctantly and tend to block progress, the stereotyped "disgruntled postal worker" being the most obvious example. Facilitators do not resist change, aren't people who "don't want to be bothered," and won't feel "put upon" by the need to work. They tend to stick out from those who would prefer to complain about the way things are rather than seek ways to change them.

For the most part, facilitators are the people who make up the ranks of middle management who, in Alvin Toffler's words, "are accustomed to straight-line solutions to straight-forward problems." If they are ambitious, they can move up through the ranks without necessarily ever becoming real achievers in their own right. Indeed, many successful companies have continued on a standard, nondeveloping path for years, sometimes decades, led by a nonachieving facilitator who understood the procedure book and stuck to it, riding its gentle wave all the way to the top of a major corporation.

In 1971, Reuben Mark was President of Colgate Venezuela. He was a bright and personable young man. When he made presentations to Hank Carpenter, then the president of Colgate International, and me (as vice president for Latin America and Canada), he was always marvelously "buttoned up." Even at the airport, he outshone the other managers by having the limousine that met Hank and me drive right to the airplane steps. (I later found out that Reuben had "purchased" a membership in the Venezuelan police force and thus had "run of the airport" privileges.) Nevertheless, things almost went wrong.

Reuben's well-organized competitive data-collection team had discovered that Procter & Gamble's Crest was soon to be awarded the seal of approval by the Venezuelan Dental Association. Colgate's seal of approval, which Reuben had been pursuing assiduously, would not be granted for at least a year. When the American Dental Association had similarly rewarded Crest before Colgate in the United States, Crest had made major inroads into Colgate's market share. Reuben, quite correctly, was worried. Colgate toothpaste sales represented the better part of his business.

In an attempt to defend his business, Reuben developed defensive plans based on beefed-up advertising and extra couponing. They were sound enough, indeed straight from the procedure book. But Reuben realized that they were wholly inadequate for this sort of competitive onslaught. Hank Carpenter stated forthrightly that he believed that Reuben's plan was insufficient. The problem was that Reuben didn't know what else to do. There was nothing in the "procedure book" to guide him. He was at an impasse.

It was a young local product manager (I am ashamed to admit I have no remembrance of his name) who came up with the complete answer.

It was simple. At his suggestion, Colgate funded something called the Pan American Dental Association, headquartered in an eight-by-ten-foot office in Guatemala City, the brainchild of a lone Guatemalan dentist. (I have often wondered cynically whether, perchance, the idea was given to him by the young Venezuelan manager. At the time, I did not ask!)

Now that Reuben knew what to do, he was again in charge. Quickly, his staff created a logo for the organization and started a research program. The right to use the logo was granted to Colgate throughout Latin America. Within weeks, every tube of Venezuelan Colgate carried the crest of the Pan American Dental Association. That was that. Were Crest to launch its toothpaste later with the approval of the "mere" Venezuelan Dental Association, they would look second best in the face of Colgate's endorsement by the multinational "Pan American Dental Association." As a result, Crest was never launched. Reuben's career was accelerated because I was justified in promoting him to run Colgate, Canada. I can only hope that, before he left Venezuela, Reuben in turn promoted the young man who had saved him.

Once in Canada, Reuben again did a commendable job running Colgate there—always according to the rules. But sales were not growing fast enough, and the rules were not flexible enough. Once more, Reuben had no idea what to do.

This time, I was able to save the situation by taking the simple but, at Colgate, unprecedented step of acquiring a large competitor, the John Houston Company, and merging it into Colgate. Reuben did an exemplary job of organizing the merger, and was promoted to Colgate's New York headquarters as vice president of marketing services, a staff position. Here he shone, as I expected he would, because such staff positions in large corporations require a facilitator, not an achiever. Marketing services works strictly to support the line managers. And it is usually among them that, if you are lucky, the exceptional individuals are to be found. Thus, Reuben was in a perfect spot for his particular abilities.

Gradually, Reuben Mark moved up the ladder. By 1980, he knew more about every aspect of how Colgate worked than any other person in the company. He was bright, personable, cheerful, healthy, and witty. His personal charisma and sense of humor delighted the directors and Keith Crane, the retiring CEO. And so Reuben Mark, a classic facilitator, became president, chairman, and

CEO of the $6 billion Colgate-Palmolive multinational. He had earned that position with loyalty, tenacity, and competence, not by achievement.

At this point, the Colgate story becomes almost a case study of what happens when facilitators, not high achievers, run things at the top. The story is well worth telling both for itself and as a warning to investors.

During the 1970s, a brilliant entrepreneurial Englishman, David Foster, ran Colgate. He was shy, rather chubby, unpredictable, and often not especially friendly. But withal, he achieved brilliantly. When I joined Colgate in 1971, its sales were $1.3 billion and its profits $45 million. I still treasure a gold tie clip given to me, which has a 2 inscribed on it. That was to commemorate the year our sales topped $2.0 billion. By the time I left in 1980, sales of such lowly levels were achieved in just a few months. Annual revenues that year reached $5.1 billion. Profits were up to an impressive $173 million. In a scant five years, David Foster, leading a tiny band of us, his loyal followers, had built the company at an extraordinary rate.

In 1982, David was asked to resign. For two years the company marked time under an interim president, Keith Crane. Then, in 1984, Reuben Mark became CEO, the best person Colgate had for the job: charming, quick-witted, exceedingly knowledgeable about the company—and a facilitator through and through.

For eight solid years, the company made no financial progress. The figures speak for themselves: no sales growth, no profit growth:

	1983 (Base Year)	1984	1985	1986	1987	1988	1989	1990	1991
Sales ($ Billions)	4.9	4.9	4.5	5.0	5.6	4.7	5.1	5.7	5.1
Profit ($ Millions)	198.0	54.0*	168.0	178.0**	1.0	153.0	280.0	321.0	125.0

* In 1984, the year Mark took over, he reduced profits with the result that the following year profits looked better (although not as good as the year before his arrival).

** In 1986, seeking to do better than the prior year, the company pushed for profits and then took a "one-shot" write-off in 1987!

Then, at last, Mark (or perhaps his directors) figured something had to be done. But only achievers build. *Mark, a wonderfully competent, "by-the-book" administrator, was not of that type. To raise profits, he didn't build, he cut. Sales grew from their 1991 level of $5.1 billion, aided by an acquisition and currency variations favorable to Colgate, to $7.5 billion in 1994, about a 50 percent increase. But expenses were cut drastically so that profits rose to $580 million, an astonishing 460 percent increase.*

But, of course, cutting without achievement can't work for long. Lower spending means more vulnerability to every high-achieving competitor. As one Colgate insider phrased it, "You can't keep cutting your way to glory." Inevitably, in 1995, earnings tumbled by a disastrous "one-time" charge of $369 million. Naturally, as The Delaney Report *wrote, the "latest move by Mark puts Colgate-Palmolive staffers in doldrums." In 1996 and 1997, sales and profits rose again to new, healthier-than-ever levels. And in early 1998, Colgate announced a brilliant new product, a toothpaste called Colgate Total that fights gingivitis as well as tooth decay. The company put an unprecedented amount of advertising behind the product. Will it succeed? It is too early to say. If it does, perhaps Reuben Mark has at last moved himself to the level of a future achiever. If* *not, the past two years of solid results will be followed by another massive write-off, until eventually some new exceptional individual acquires control of the company—and business starts once again to build.*

One final comment on the Colgate case: When the company announced that 1995 profits would be back down to the 1989 level or less, The Wall Street Journal *reported that the "massive restructuring plan drew cheers on Wall Street." There were also cheers, at least muted ones, when David Foster was forced out. Yet the facts and all common sense show how much more effective Foster and his team were than their successors. Here again, we are faced with an instructive example of how we tend to value mediocrity and decry achievement.*

Facilitators like Reuben Mark are vital to the success of a business struggling to achieve. If you are attempting the impossible, facilitators will help and assist you. They never drag their feet. But they are not achievers. That is a special talent. As Peter Drucker explains, we need facilitators because we just don't have enough achievers to go around:

> If effectiveness were a gift people were born with, the way they are born with a gift for music or an eye for painting, we would be in bad shape, for we know that only a small minority is born with great gifts in any one of these areas. We would, therefore, be reduced to trying to spot people with high potential of effectiveness early and to train them as best we know to develop their talent. But we could hardly hope to find enough people for the executive tasks of modern society this way.

I agree completely that many of the executive tasks of our society have to be executed by effective facilitators. But I suspect that America's greatest authority on management does not recognize that it *always* takes a few people, a "small minority born with great gifts," to allow a company to achieve a truly outstanding success. Only men and women striving for personal excellence can actually crank up the engine of a new business or strike out in a bold new direction. These people will always be the essential catalysts, training the capable but underachieving people around them and elevating them to at least a reasonable level of effectiveness. Facilitators may indeed excel in their duties, but they have to be inspired and led if they are to create movement where there is none.

Achievement is not a solitary activity. Both Alexander the Great and Catherine the Great had an army of foot soldiers who carried out their impossible, world-conquering plans. And Alexander prayed to an army of gods to boot, all adduced to his cause from the peoples he conquered. Similarly, all exceptional individuals who succeed know that, without facilitators, their own excellence cannot be fully exploited.

Thus, we face the interesting near anomaly that, without the energizing effect of high achievers, facilitators will not be motivated to achieve very much at all; whereas without the facilitator to "do the work," high achievers would have little chance to implement their plans. Achievers' mobilizing leadership is the key here; as in other matters, the efforts of the exceptional individuals are the starting point in achievement.

Every idea or vision needs to be made into something of a crusade by the high achievers to encourage the facilitators to strive. So important is this motivation that, in many companies, even the Deity is invoked.

"God will give you the strength to succeed," Mary Kay executives insist. "He wants you to be rich."

Facilitators by themselves succeed only in the small

things. They participate but do not generate the apparently inevitable annual growth of their companies; they make only small changes in already successful products or strategies. The theory of small wins discussed previously is made for them, designed so that they can slap each other on the back and congratulate themselves and one another on small successes. In the process, facilitators often gather prestige, pensions, and paunches—but they cannot achieve personal excellence.

On the other hand, by rarely making small mistakes, facilitators are often in danger of making massive ones. While they are adept at keeping the furnace stoked and turning off the lights before they leave, facilitators may be made redundant when the need for major structural change in business direction arises. Indeed, their own businesses tend to crush them. "High novelty . . . demands precisely the kind of executive skills that traditional bureaucracies crush," Toffler assures us.

Such massive changes became frequent, to the point of being commonplace, in the United States over the past several years. They are largely the result of three separate, albeit interconnected, circumstances: the huge debt loads corporations assumed to buy each other out; the general laziness that came with the easy success that American industry enjoyed after much of the rest of the developed world was destroyed by World War II; and partly, as we have discussed, the reliance on the facilitators and on the techniques of business, rather than on exceptional individuals capable of using the facilitators (and the techniques) to implement their dreams.

Caught in such vicious corporate downdrafts, facilitators' careers can be destroyed. They usually lack the imagination and the resiliency to withstand structural change, they lack power to influence these events, and they even lack the stomachs to fight. Facilitators may be bright and well educated, carry MBAs from the best business schools in the country, be perfectly trained in administration, expert at number-crunching, masters of business theory, and beautifully mannered, yet by happenstance they can, and often do, fail totally as the environment around them no longer values their input.

A few years ago, a bright young manager with a fresh new MBA from the Harvard Business School was sent to Brazil to reorganize the subsidiary of a major American consumer goods company. He was given a very clear mandate to clean up the mess, and precise instructions on how to do it.

At that time, the mid-1970s, Brazil was in chaos, enmeshed in a debilitating series of military coups. Inflation was rampant and consumer optimism nonexistent. As for the company he was supposed to reorganize, well, the young manager found it to be perilously close to bankruptcy. The previous manager, ironically the first Brazilian to hold the position, had been dishonest and libertine. Although for quite a while he had covered his tracks well, he was most thoroughly corrupt. Apparently in return for a variety of payoffs from local manufacturers, he had launched a series of new products no one wanted. But he had sold them on credit. So they remained, piled high in retail stores, unsold, unsalable, and, much worse, unpaid for by the retailers. As triple-digit inflation exploded, the value of every one of those receivables collapsed. The company, facing this backbreaking financial loss, was on the brink of catastrophe, led there with remarkable vigor and flair by the new manager's predecessor. The head office in New York had an inkling of the problem—which is why they had sent the young manager there—but no idea of its full extent.

The new young manager moved into this disastrous situation

*with enormous energy to do precisely what he'd been told. He fired
the sales manager for stealing, dismissed the dozen or so decorative
young ladies who seemed to do nothing but preen at their desks, cut
his losses on the unsold inventories by deep discounting. He bor-
rowed money at half the earlier rates—but not from the previous
president's moneylender friends—and sold a large chunk of un-
developed real estate in Rio de Janeiro, which he discovered was co-
owned by the former president's cousin. Then, cautiously, he
introduced a few proven products from the parent corporation.
Slowly, the business turned. Then, helped by a temporary improvement in Brazil's economy, it suddenly boomed. Within three years,
the business was reasonably profitable and the young man was
earning accolades from his superiors back in the United States.*

*For five years, as the Brazilian economy worsened again, the
new manager, no longer so new or so young, held the company in
the black. Profits were not impressive, but there were no losses, either. The head office, while no longer wiring congratulations, remained satisfied and supportive.*

*Then, at last, the situation in Brazil changed permanently. The
military government departed, a fledgling democracy took hold, and,
although it never achieved stability, Brazil began to grow explosively. Local corporations often grew at 25 percent a year or more.
Real estate prices skyrocketed. Millionaires sprouted like mushrooms
after rain. At one point in the 1980s, the city of São Paulo was
completing 100 apartment buildings and 100 kilometers of road
daily!*

*However, the young manager's company was now settled into
a comfortable market niche, well staffed, conservatively financed,
and respectably predictable. The almost middle-aged manager was
now fluent in Portuguese, a happily married father of two, and
socially established. Every day he remembered how his conservatism
had been praised. Often he boasted how he had saved the company
by pulling back on a glut of unsuccessful new product introductions.*

When younger men urged him to move more aggressively to take advantage of Brazil's quantum leap forward in opportunity, he refused to push the envelope. He preferred instead to continue to do what he had been trained to do. Facilitator that he was, he simply did not realize that the bandwagon had changed direction and that the band itself was playing a completely different tune. In the absence of any new instructions, he continued to adhere to the old.

To his utter surprise, he was asked to resign.

Frequently, of course, facilitators continue to succeed because nothing changes and the path upon which they have been set continues, by a happy coincidence, to be an appropriate one. Then the facilitators act in the same way as do the achievers. Then they are viewed, as the achievers are, as having greatness. But of course they are benefiting from the ambient success; they are not its instigators. As T. S. Eliot put it in *Murder in the Cathedral,* "The last temptation is the greatest treason, to do the right deed for the wrong reason." While such managers may eventually retire wreathed with accolades and blessed with wealth, it's important to note that there are stark differences between the roles of facilitators and achievers. Facilitators are a part of the support system; they are not the creators of the system.

DRONES ARE THE ENEMIES OF ACHIEVEMENT

If exceptional individuals (as the term implies) are rare, and facilitators infrequent, then the majority of the daily workforce is made up of what we might call, rather unkindly, drones. Like facilitators, drones follow instructions. Unlike facilitators, however, they do so with just enough reluctance to become an actual impediment to progress. Where facilitators do not know how to initiate change and therefore stay on a single path until pushed onto a new one, drones actually resist being pushed and complain whiningly when they are. While not refusing the new direction (only achievers of commendable vigor will refuse to move onto a new path if they think it ill advised), drones will resist in the business equivalent of passive-aggressiveness. Thus, although they will reluctantly implement a change, they will burden it with a cartload of explanations, excuses, justifications, and doubts. Their goal, usually unconscious, will be to insure that action is slow at best, and often entirely stymied. These rather telling characteristics make drones readily recognizable in any business.

Drones may be against change and represent an actual interference with progress, but they need not be, by their nature, fools or juniors. As long as the business goes well, it is likely to pull its drones along with it, mildly dissatisfied, but successful in spite of themselves. Sometimes they even take on the protective coloration of facilitators and accept part of the facilitators' roles—as long as things are going well and there is no reason or push for change. Their true colors only emerge when change becomes desirable.

Michael was an experienced group product manager in charge of four of his company's brands with aggregate sales of almost $50 million. He seemed to be a first-class man, a delightful and charming person, always well dressed and thoroughly informed. His job was important, but not central, to the firm's well-being.

When Rhonda joined the firm as vice president of marketing, overseeing Michael and several other managers, she noticed over the first few weeks that none of the projects Michael reported about in staff meetings seemed to be moving forward. However, nothing seemed particularly wrong, and Rhonda had a number of other higher-priority projects to worry about. Nevertheless, she was intrigued by one of Michael's undertakings, perhaps his most important one, namely to bring out a line of men's toiletries under the name of a world-famous New York restaurant. Such a line, merchandised initially to the restaurant's large, nationwide mailing list, would position the products with precisely the right sort of prestige and glamour. Consequently, on hearing of the project initially, Rhonda immediately expressed enthusiasm and, a few weeks later, she invited Michael into her office to discuss his progress.

Rhonda was quite surprised when she heard that Michael had not yet actually talked to the restaurant about the idea.

"Why not?" she wanted to know.

"Previous management turned it down," Michael explained. "They didn't like the idea."

"But I said I did."

"Yes, but I wasn't sure you really meant it. I was waiting to chat with you about it in more detail. After all, we'll only get one chance at this. I don't want to blow it."

Biting her lip to contain her impatience, Rhonda considered the circumstances. She had to admit that her enthusiasm had been right at the start of her tenure. Maybe Michael was right to be careful. "Very well," she agreed. "But now you know that I share your enthusiasm. So let's move!" And to underline her enthusiasm, Rhonda followed up the discussion with a series of encouraging memos, positive responses to Michael's meeting summaries, and occasional inquiries about his progress. Then, assuming that this would be sufficient, she left Michael alone while she dealt with several more immediate problems besieging her.

Nevertheless, a year later, Michael's restaurant project still hadn't moved forward. He had had several lengthy meetings with the restaurant's owners, who seemed mildly interested. But as Michael reported, he would "have to work even harder to convince them."

A few more months passed. Still no action resulted. Neither success nor failure. Nothing.

At the end of two years, having dealt with her higher-priority projects, Rhonda looked more carefully at Michael's efforts. And she was appalled. For two years Michael had initiated nothing at all. The restaurant project was at a standstill. Worse, nothing else had happened, either. Michael's product managers, his department, even his desk, were always in perfect shape. But it was the perfection that comes only from standing absolutely still. Other brand managers had developed and launched new products, had conquered new channels of distribution, had opened new markets. Some had enjoyed great success; others had been forced to deal with failures. Michael had done nothing at all.

It took Rhonda about a week to merge Michael's brand group into another department. Michael, who had "done nothing wrong," was not fired. But his job having been eliminated, Rhonda had no choice but to ask him to leave the firm!

This is not an isolated circumstance. Drones exist at all levels of business, and in virtually all large companies.

My father was president of a small but respected company that had a remarkable record of accomplishment at creating successful, profitable new products. One of these products was a new aerosol system, which he offered to a large manufacturer of nasal decongestants. It seemed the perfect fit. The new system worked dry rather than with liquid and released no fluorocarbons into the atmosphere. Thus, it was more environmentally sound than anything on the market at that time. Moreover, the system could be manufactured less expensively, and thus sold at a greater profit than other products. All the patent applications were in order, which would have inhibited initial competition. It seemed to be a perfect win-win situation.

*I asked my father if I could accompany him to the presentation
meeting with the company's president.*

*"Of course," my father agreed readily. "But don't get your
hopes up."*

"Why not?" I demanded.

*"You'll see," my father said enigmatically. "These things
rarely lead anywhere."*

*The meeting went very well. My father made a clear and per-
suasive presentation. The listeners were visibly impressed. I was
delighted . . . until, to my astonishment and dismay, the president
of the company replied with a curt, "No, thank you." He then
explained, "Your product would seem to be substantially better
than ours and would, therefore, tend to cannibalize our present
business. We would not be interested in bringing out a new product
that could replace sales of our existing products."*

Even successful companies have to suffer drones, sometimes in high places. Fortunately, the drones are largely in-
active, representing ballast that slows down the boat rather
than an anchor designed to actively stop it. They would not
be drones, of course, if they were that active. Thus, the negative impact of many drones can easily be offset by the positive impact of a smaller number of facilitators, and quite a
small number of exceptional individuals. It is the right ratios
of these three that makes the companies Collins and Porras
call visionary.

Managers who strive for personal excellence will find
ways to lead the facilitators to action. They will nurture,
cajole, and manage them into a concerted drive toward
achievement. At the same time, they will find a significant
cadre of drones in their organizations who are unarousa-
ble. If they are in positions that require any more than
routine repetition of what works, achievers will be forced

to find a way to let them go. Such drones are truly dead weight.

Personal excellence has its own motor force, and a logic that drives its possessor. One part of that logic is that, while facilitators can be motivated to achieve action, drones, who cannot, must go.

10

MONEY AND MARKETING

New ventures need money. They also need to establish themselves in whatever field they are entering by marketing their concept or product effectively. Typically, most entrepreneurs will focus too much on the first need and not enough on the latter. The exceptional individual should necessarily consider the demands of each stage of development and not become obsessed solely with raising funds.

Still, money *is* needed. Thus, one of the main responsibilities that any high-achieving entrepreneur faces near the start of a new venture is to raise funds. Contrary to popular belief, raising money is usually not of the essence in starting a new venture. That is because, while it is almost always one of the paramount needs, money *is* available. The right idea with the right management—and an exceptional individual to lead the enterprise—*will* be funded and get off the ground. An estimated 600,000 new ventures open their doors annually. And every one of them, by hook or by crook, finds the minimum funds it needs.

There are almost as many ways the exceptional individual can raise funds as there are ventures that need them. Most often, at the very start of a new venture, funding comes from the entrepreneur's own savings, credit cards, second mort-gages, or future benefits (e.g. pensions).

After the start-up, most entrepreneurs find themselves casting about for ways to raise money from strangers. "Going public," generating private placements, instituting limited partnership arrangements, seeking government funding, tapping into private venture capitalists, obtaining loans from suppliers or customers, financing inventory and receivables from factors—these are just a few of the basic fund-raising techniques open to the start-up entrepreneur. In the end, one way or another, almost magically it sometimes seems, the money comes.

However, although it is true that profitable businesses rarely die because of the lack of cash, it is also true that raising funds is terribly time-consuming and difficult. For one thing, there are so many possible sources, and there is no way of differentiating in advance among the many who might pro-vide the funds from the few who actually will provide them. For another, the task of raising the money often involves selling the benefits of a product or service that has not yet been perfected or fully tested.

Worse, raising money is, in itself, essentially nonproduc-tive; it is merely a prerequisite to future productive, profit-generating activity. Thus, exceptional individuals are not necessarily ideal fund-raisers. They want to be doing, not merely preparing to do. Raising funds is yet one more of those unfortunately essential tasks they have to learn to han-dle effectively if they are to succeed in implementing their higher ambitions. Not surprisingly, the most tenacious and hungry of them do just that.

A successful young marketing man whom I shall call Jefferson Blackmore broke his leg while jogging the streets of Palo Alto, Cal-

ifornia, one summer afternoon. It was a difficult multiple fracture that required a weeklong hospital stay. An athletic young man who had already held a number of marketing positions in start-up health-care companies, Jefferson found himself sulking in miserable immobility, broken leg encased in a cast extended high in the air.

As he lay in bed, impatient, uncomfortable, and partially sedated, his college friend Harry stopped by to wish him well. Harry was one of the slower-talking, faster-thinking men in California. A private entrepreneur and promotor, Harry was skilled at ''putting people together'' for their mutual benefit. He never neglected to pinch off a small piece of the resultant action for himself.

''How does one raise money, Harry?'' Jefferson asked. He had been fantasizing about the new business concept he had been planning for several weeks.

''With difficulty!'' Harry said facetiously. Then, sincerely, he added, ''Wall Street for a public company. Venture capitalists for a private one—if you've got a winning concept. An 'angel' if you are lucky enough to know one who's interested in the business you want to finance. Bank loans if you have collateral. Or potential suppliers or customers.'' In a paragraph, Harry had covered the options.

''Do you know any venture capitalists?'' Jefferson asked. The question was rhetorical. Harry knew people at every level of society. He had many relatives in unusual places.

''Do you have an idea for a business?'' Harry asked.

Jefferson looked silently back at him.

''Of course, you do.'' Harry grinned after quickly answering his own question. Harry knew his friend.

They talked awhile. In spite of his sedated state, Jefferson's enthusiasm for his new concept came through. So did the supporting facts. It came as no surprise to Harry that Jefferson had done his homework.

''Tell you what,'' Harry promised as he was leaving. ''I'll think about it. Probably introduce you to someone who could help.''

"When?" Jefferson pushed.

"Oh, I don't know. One of these days," Harry answered, refusing to be pinned down.

But Harry was never as casual as he seemed. And here he smelled a profit opportunity. So the very next day in came Harry, pulling behind him a man whose name and aristocratic face were well known to anyone who ever read the business pages.

Although hot and suffering in his cast, and now even more sedated against the pain, Jefferson nevertheless recognized the man instantly. Here was a potential investor who had amassed a vast fortune in companies very similar to the one Jefferson was developing. And there lay Jefferson, in traction, trying to smile, realizing that he hadn't shaved or brushed his teeth, and that he had removed his pajama top because of the heat.

"Jefferson, I'm sure you know who this is," Harry said, lifting his arm with a dramatic flourish. Then, turning to his guest, he added, "Bill, this man in the cast is my friend, Jefferson Blackmore. He is one of the most dynamic young businessmen on the West Coast. And I think he's got a good idea you ought to hear."

Bill, looking down at Jefferson more with pity than enthusiasm, merely grunted.

Yet, as it turned out, that was the decisive first step in the founding of Jefferson's new biotechnology venture. It was an unusual way to begin a business relationship.

"That first day, how did you decide I was worth supporting?" Jefferson asked Bill a few years later. By that time, Jefferson's company was a glorious success and the men had become firm friends. "Surely I must have been pretty incoherent."

"Utterly!" Bill agreed. "But my, you were so enthusiastic! And I figured that anyone who could give me a fifteen-minute lecture, even a rather garbled one, while hanging almost upside down from pulleys, half drugged, and in obvious pain must be worth some-

thing. Actually, my only concern was whether you'd recover enough to get into business at all. You sure looked terrible.''

''You checked?''

''Of course. The nurse said, 'He'll be back at work in three weeks. He's far too big a pain in the ass to stay here!' ''

Of course entrepreneurs need more than good contacts and enthusiasm to start up a new company. And investors look for more than just an exciting idea. They also want a sensible and safe business base, a well-thought-out growth plan, and a manager or a group of managers who know their field and have a track record of success in it. But if they are clever and experienced investors, above all they want a dynamic, personally excellent exceptional individual to lead the business to success.

Even then, however, success is not automatic. In this respect, Jefferson's experience is instructive. The adventure began after Jefferson was released from the hospital. Recovering sufficiently, he grew restless to begin the greatest challenge of his life. He was enormously energized. He felt as if he were about to enter an Olympic competition he had been training for most of his life. And Bill had promised him just enough seed money to get started.

Jefferson's company was founded on a simple idea whose success had been demonstrated many times in other industries. His goal was to apply mass marketing to the field of biotechnology, then still in its infancy. Many of its leading players were "mad scientist" types who didn't think much about selling, promoting, or positioning their products. It was a bit like the beginning of the personal computer era, Jefferson observed. The leading edge of technology was far ahead of the products, and those were far more advanced than their marketing. Jefferson felt that, correctly positioned and sold to consumers, many of the new biotech concepts could become vastly important. As a group, they would literally revolutionize our health care. So he set out to take advantage of this enormous future potential.

We must now define the word *marketing* as Jefferson Blackmore understood it. The definition that appealed to him was that "marketing is the art and science of persuading more consumers than you can talk to personally to use your product or service consistently."

THE SCIENCE OF MARKETING

The science of marketing a product is crucial. It consists in the first place of developing a product that, at least in one significant way, is superior to any other product on the market. But technical superiority alone is usually not sufficient. Thus, the science of marketing also encompasses "positioning" the new (or sometimes an existing) product into its market in such a way that its technical advantages are meaningful. (A detergent with a more refined fragrance probably has no place in a commercial laundry, but might be very desirably positioned for consumer washing delicate garments by hand.)

Most great marketing successes have, at their beginning, a genuine product advantage. The compact disc did not replace the record album because of a great advertising blitz by the music industry. It succeeded because its sound quality was superior. Japanese cars and German automobiles gained sales in world markets versus American cars because of finer engineering and styling. Ivory Soap was successful not mainly because of the famous advertising slogans "99$\frac{44}{100}$%

Pure," and "It Floats," but rather because Ivory was the first wholly consistent pure soap and, by golly, it did float. The Xerox copier, Post-it notes, the IBM computer, Tampax, spandex, Windows '95, M&M's, Rolex watches, Crest toothpaste, Mont Blanc fountain pens, safety glass, light beer, and diet colas were all, at their outset, better consumer products in at least one significant respect.

But positioning is important too. Mont Blanc pens have to be status symbols as well as superb writing instruments in order to justify their price. Windows '95 is merely an upgrade, but it has been successfully positioned as a huge breakthrough, a "must-have" piece of technology. Light beer failed dismally at first because it was positioned to women and to men on diets. It became successful when it was repositioned to macho beer drinkers with the not-so-subliminal message "You can drink more of this."

Sometimes, too, the science of marketing results in a product that is lower in price. An equally good product that costs less than competing brands is, in that one respect, a "better" product. Of course new and better products are rapidly imitated. However, few of the imitators, if they have no technical advantages of their own, ever become as commercially successful as the original. The same is true for business concepts. Federal Express, Wal-Mart stores, the Body Shop boutiques, Roto-Rooter drain cleaners, McDonald's restaurants, and many more had a distinctly better product that offered people an enhanced real and perceived value. Although today their competitors are just as good, in each of these cases the first introducer of the concept remains the category leader.

Similarly, most major product marketing failures—and failures do quickly fade from memory—were not so much the result of improper marketing as of ill-conceived or poor products. The Edsel was the most famous marketing disaster in the automobile industry. It failed because people simply didn't like the car. Remember Coca-Cola's attempt to reformulate its original formula? More bad science. IBM's attempt to replace MS/DOS with its own operating system, OS/2, was a dismal and expensive failure. Does anyone recall the other competing home video formats, all of which were supplanted by the VHS? Remember Vote toothpaste? Daisie snack foods? How about the Yugo? Does anyone remember Tressy dolls, which unsuccessfully made a run on the huge market for Barbie dolls? These products, and many businesses with similarly flawed concepts, went the way of the saber-toothed tiger because they lacked a compelling product advantage. Or, if they had one (after all Tressy's hair did grow!), they failed to position it so that consumers viewed it as a real advantage. The science was not there.

THE ART OF MARKETING

The *art* of marketing is to understand what about the putatively superior product consumers really appreciate (as distinct from the superior product itself which is developed through the *science* of marketing), and then to find a way of trumpeting that advantage and making sure that consumers know about it and appreciate what they know. An inferior product or a product that neither in fact nor in positioning can show any points of superiority, or a product that has a point of superiority that too few people know about or believe in, will surely fail. But marketing is important. There are many examples of products that are only marginally superior to existent competitors, which nonetheless achieve substantial success because of good marketing.

———————

Many years ago, right at the start of my career, I was promoted by my employer, Procter & Gamble, Canada, to the exalted position of brand manager in charge of their old-line product, Oxydol. To try to resuscitate the brand (which had been declining for years), my predecessors had added a color-safe bleach to the product. Sales had continued to decline without even a blip of improvement.

At the suggestion of my boss, I conducted a market research study to find out why consumers weren't buying our product. After all, as our advertising correctly claimed, it was superior for any clothing that needed the stain-removal power of a bleach.

"We just don't believe it," our interviewees told us. "You say you put bleach in, but if you do, it's probably only in trace quantities. And by the way, we never believe any advertising."

That's when I came up with one of the few new ideas of my life! I arranged for about 5 percent of the Oxydol to be colored green. The resultant mixture was speckled, the first speckled detergent ever marketed.

Of course, the green detergent contained no more bleach than the white detergent. But our advertising explained that "the green speckles show you that there's bleach in Oxydol."

Now consumers believed our story. Oxydol's market share sky-rocketed.

The art of marketing is important, and can sometimes be decisive. Pepsi Cola is a "me too" product to its core, with hardly any "science" advantage over Coca-Cola, the originator of the cola concept. Yet it has grown to almost Coke's size by a constant round of innovative and upbeat advertising and promotion.

Thus, the art of marketing can be summarized as the technique by which the manufacturer describes a product's "scientific" advantage to be particularly appealing to the consumer, and then disseminates that description in every possible way. The product's description is to be used in packaging, in in-store merchandising, and of course in all media advertising.

So let's return to the story of Jefferson. He had decided to use the science and art of marketing to build himself a significant position in the biotech field.

In the world of biotechnology, in its earlier years, few companies had anything similar to an integrated marketing program. A few of the mammoth drug companies ran generic or institutional advertising campaigns, but not about biotechnology. That was still considered a bit "out there," and few of the institutional giants who had cautiously brought out a few test products wanted to advertise their involvement.

The few mad scientist types who actually had products that were of demonstrable value had begun some embarrassingly simpleminded advertising campaigns. But they lacked the know-how (and usually the interest) to follow through. Thus, Jefferson Blackmore's new company, Biological & Technology Marketing Services, was formed to combine the marketing efforts for several noncompetitive companies under one roof. However, instead of working for all cash fees, Jefferson decided he would work for half price, taking the other half of his pay in shares of stock in each of the companies he served.

Jefferson's idea was grand enough to meet the first requirement of possible backers, namely the chance of an impressive return on their investment. But before they actually laid out money to finance his venture, the backers naturally wanted to know exactly what Jefferson had planned. Laboriously, for there is no other way, he wrote a full business plan.

The second step, and probably the most important one for investors, was for Jefferson to add "security" to the idea. Harry had interested a number of potential investors, but Jefferson's good ideas alone were not financeable. In response to that need, Jefferson negotiated marketing agreements with a number of biotechnology companies who had already expressed an interest and signed them to long-term contracts. He was able to achieve this rather impressive feat by giving his new clients a small interest in Biological & Technology Marketing Services. He also proposed that part of his investors' money be used to buy a small office building in the Santa Clara Valley, within a few miles of each of the fledgling companies. "You can't lose on real estate," he assured them.

At last, the investors were reassured enough to put up the money, and Jefferson had what he needed to get his business underway. Immediately, he faced a million problems. They came at him so fast that they all blurred together. Sleep became a luxury. His life seemed to be an unending workday. But he rose to the challenges as they appeared, and felt himself growing stronger professionally as he struggled.

Getting a business started is a lot easier than keeping one going through its transition to maturity. Opening a business merely requires an idea, a short-term plan of action, and enough resourcefulness and energy to make it happen. Keeping it on track requires both a viable long-term business plan strong enough to withstand everything from competitive reaction to plain bad luck, and an overachiever's stamina, perseverance, determination, intelligence, and hunger.

11

BUILDING

Building a new and vigorous motive force onto any established field isn't easy. This is best exemplified by the continuing example of Jefferson Blackmore. While he was trying to push forward, the rest of the world seemed bent on holding him back. As I have discussed before, the trauma of change and growth is uncomfortable, and thus people resist. Ironically, large changes—the move from an industrial to an information society, the quest to understand the makeup of the human gene, the solution to the world food and raw material "crises"—usually move faster than we anticipate. That is because they become the norm and are no longer felt as change (even though the change they involve is fundamental). Rather, it is the relatively small changes that people understand and therefore resist.

As Jefferson tried to move his company forward, the resistance he faced (in physics terms, the "moment of inertia," if you will) made him, like so many entrepreneurs before him, lose patience with his colleagues. His entire life was focused on moving his business forward. So how could they "waste their time" attending irrelevant parties and social events? Friends began asking him why he never called anymore. His old tennis partner vainly tried to get him interested in the club tournament. His girlfriend couldn't understand why, when she invited him for a home-cooked meal, Jefferson always appeared late and left early. Even at work, Jefferson was always behind in his latest priority, slow to fulfill his assurances, overworked and irritable.

Gradually, Jefferson was learning about the third key requirement sought by investors, investment bankers, even corporate managers: namely, the need for a strong group of supporting managers.

Jefferson slowly (or so it seemed to him) assembled a first-rate marketing team. It consisted of a top-notch creative director, a computer programmer/designer, a senior sales executive, and a crack financial manager to hold the entire package together. These people, two women and two men, were all conversant with both science and marketing. And they worked well together. Within months, they began to attract clients and develop a series of innovative marketing campaigns.

Unfortunately, because Jefferson had not been able to move fast enough at the start, although business was looking good, the company was behind its original forecasts. The investors were therefore pressuring him for higher and quicker returns. To make matters worse, a recession had hit, slowing Jefferson's customers—and therefore his business, too.

Unwisely, Jefferson told his investors rather abruptly that their demands were unrealistic. They pointed out that they were only asking for what he had promised. An argument ensued. The result was that the investors lost much of their confidence in Jefferson. And the result of that was that they started to withhold working capital at crucial times. To compensate, Jefferson had to dig deeply into his own pockets. To do so, he took out a series of short-term loans at the local bank.

But the mistrust grew. Just three years after he had founded his company, billings had exceeded $10 million per year and the company was well in the black. But Jefferson's loans were due and the only way he could pay them was to sell his share of the company to the investors. They were delighted, feeling confident that they no longer needed Jefferson. Indeed, they felt so confident that they were not even seriously concerned when three of the four key managers working for Jefferson handed in their resignations and left with their boss.

On Jefferson's final day, he made a farewell speech to his assembled employees about the bright future of biotechnology, and of their company within it. He thanked all his friends, for they were all his friends by then, and generously wished his successor good luck. He emphasized that he was convinced that the company was based on a concept so sound it would prosper for a hundred years. He even lauded his successor, a first-class executive with sound administrative and personnel skills from a Madison Avenue agency. Then he departed amidst the cheers and tears of his employees.

What actually happened after that was totally unexpected both to Jefferson and to the investors. Instead of continuing to concentrate on marketing the biotechnology products, the new CEO began ''diversifying'' to market other types of products and services. Billings grew for a while, and the investors congratulated themselves. But it took only a few short months for the staff, nearly all new, to become confused. The agency's vaunted focus on biotech marketing began to erode. Now they claimed to be expert at everything. Existing clients felt the lack of expertise; new clients wouldn't believe what they were told. Only the company's accounting and administrative departments, which had always been understaffed because of lack of money, now worked really well with augmented staffs. They were able to report ever more rapidly and accurately the failing fortunes of the business.

Less than two years after Jefferson Blackmore left the company, Biological & Technology Marketing Services was forced into Chapter

11 bankruptcy. It had taken less time to ruin the company than to build it.

In retrospect, the fundamental reason for the failure is clear: It was not that the company diversified too soon, or made any other fundamental errors. On the contrary, broadening their client base, attracting sufficient funding, and improving administration were all good moves. Rather, they failed because the replacement of the founder and his staff of high-achieving exceptional individuals came too early in the game. The company had not created sufficient momentum to roll forward under its own weight. While Jefferson and his original team felt they were running for their lives, the facilitators who replaced them felt no such imperative. They put in an honest day's work for an honest day's pay, but no more than that. The late-night oil burned no more. New management concentrated on not making definable mistakes so that no one could be blamed for any disaster that might occur on their watch. They adopted a ''don't make waves'' philosophy in a company that had been run by guts and grit. As a result, they virtually assured its demise. It was the old story of the fox chasing the rabbit. The fox was running for his dinner, but the rabbit was running for his life. No wonder the rabbit got away. When the foxes took over Biological & Technology Marketing Services, the end was near because they were only running for their dinner.

In *Management and Machiavelli,* Antony Jay writes that successful generals, like successful business leaders, share a great urge to seize the initiative. There does come a time in a company's life when the raw creative passion and drive of the founding entrepreneur become excessive. Shaking the tree to get rid of the rotten apples is one thing; continuing to shake until the good apples are knocked down or bruised to pieces is another. When that happens, the founder must be replaced by a management team that can bring in a sense of calm and can consolidate the gains of the past. But this phase is generally short-lived. The consolidation complete, a new drive for excellence is needed. New achievers must be encouraged, new advances made.

As countless examples of entrepreneurially founded companies illustrate, start-up success requires a classic overachiever's approach. Thereafter, the high achiever may not be needed for a while if the company is well staffed with competent facilitators. But that situation lasts *only as long as the company's path to success remains straight and narrow.* If that path suddenly passes over unexpected bumps or around unforeseen curves, the facilitators will be at a loss. In that case, once again, one or more exceptional individuals will be essential to maintain the momentum.

THE DRIVE TO BUILD

In capitalistic countries, one of the traditional ways of creating action is by starting a business. We are all familiar with the rags-to-riches stories of many overachieving entrepreneurs who start businesses with only a few dollars, a vision, and a tremendous will to succeed.

Billionaire entertainment mogul David Geffen was born in Brooklyn, the son of a corset-maker. He graduated in the bottom 10 percent of his class in high school and dropped out of two colleges before he gravitated toward the entertainment business. There he had little to recommend him but his overwhelming ambition. He began working in the mail room of the giant William Morris Agency, but of course such a lowly position hardly satisfied his am-

bition. Complaining to a colleague that he was not moving forward quickly enough, he was advised to ''work with people your own age.'' His adviser may well have meant ''your own kind,'' for Geffen was not hiding the fact that he was gay even at a time when being open about that was rare and risky. Geffen decided that his own age and kind would be found in the music business, which had long fascinated him in any case.

Geffen's instinct about performers was astonishing from the very start. Eventually it became legendary. He began as a talent agent and then founded his own record company, Asylum Records. Joni Mitchell, Jackson Browne, Linda Ronstadt, and the Eagles were among the musical talents he discovered. At this period in his life, Geffen has said that he found undiscovered musical talent literally everywhere he went. Within two years, he sold Asylum Records to Warner Communications for $7 million. Geffen said it was the highest number he could think of at the time.

As a corporate entertainment superstar, working for Steve Ross at Warner, Geffen moved into the movie business, greenlighting such pictures as Oh, God! with George Burns, and Robert Towne's Personal Best. Incorrectly diagnosed as having bladder cancer, Geffen left show business and taught at UCLA and Yale for four years. But shortly after he was given a clean bill of health, Geffen jumped back into the record business by founding Geffen Records and creating one of the best informal networking systems in Hollywood. He maintains this network with nonstop telephone calls and has always stayed on top of the latest trends in music and elsewhere. The Geffen Records label became the home to such massively successful groups as Guns N' Roses and Aerosmith.

Geffen bought a one-third interest in the enormously successful play Cats, and then went on to produce such improbable hit movies as Risky Business and Beetlejuice.

In 1990, Geffen sold his record company to entertainment giant

MCA *for 10 million MCA shares, then worth $540 million. Later that year, MCA was bought out by Matsushita, making Geffen's holdings worth $710 million. This made the boy from Brooklyn a billionaire when his art collection, real estate, film, and other assets were taken into account.*

But there is more to the story than that, for Geffen is a typical example of the entrepreneurial overachiever (albeit a more than typically successful one). Today, Geffen is actively pursuing new goals as a partner with Steven Spielberg and Jeffrey Katzenberg in SKG Dreamworks.

The point of the Geffen story is to demonstrate how high achievers in entrepreneurialism are never satisfied with the success they have achieved. They are always struggling for more. In Geffen's case, he has succeeded in the music business, in films, in plays, in real estate, and is now part of Dreamworks' grand attempt at building an entirely new kind of high-tech, "talent-driven" entertainment powerhouse. In Ross Perot's case, nothing but a run for the presidency could fulfill his need for a new challenge after he had earned a few billion dollars from EDS. In Bill Gates's case, the world has yet to see what he will aim for if he completes his first goal of dominating the *entire* computer software scene.

Entrepreneurs come in all forms: standard men and women with facilitator attitudes who buy franchises and follow the franchisers' rules to the furthest detail; relatively low-level achievers who work at their concerns with competence and tenacity and generate a solid income and sometimes considerable wealth; and Geffen-esque high achievers who build new entrepreneurial worlds. Thus, entrepreneurialism is not, per se, the home of the exceptional individual.

Only outstandingly successful entrepreneurial ventures can make that claim.

THE DRIVE TO FREEDOM

Exceptional individuals driven to seek personal excellence sometimes feel forced to leave the constraining confines of big business because they seek the freedom to move forward faster. They become private entrepreneurs to accommodate their drive and ambition, their hunger.

Of course, no one knows what percentage of new businesses are started to avoid the constrictions of a large corporation, that is, by men and women who feel they *have* to run their own business because no one will let them run theirs. But a high percentage of new businesses fail relatively early in their life, and it is tempting to guess that those are the concerns that are founded by nonachievers out of their desperation to "get away" rather than for the more positive drive to build something. However, not all start-up failures are run by underachievers. Indeed, it may be even more surprising that outstanding "start-up" entrepreneurs also fail with remarkable frequency. The reason, in a nutshell, is that the characteristics needed for achievement in a start-up company are often the diametrical opposite of what it takes to succeed in running an established company. I shall deal with these issues shortly.

First, however, I would like to emphasize just how astonishing it is that most new concepts, especially those that eventually make a fundamental difference in our lives, are created by individuals, not by large companies.

This is the more astonishing because the simple fact is

that, in theory, big business is generally better equipped to recognize and then pursue opportunities than is the individual.

BIG IDEAS ARE NOT FOR BIG BUSINESS

Obviously, big business, far more than entrepreneurs, has the financial and human resources to launch new products, exploit new concepts, and change our world. Even the "moment of inertia" found in the largest corporation should be less inhibiting than the lack of strength, power, and money that an entrepreneur faces alone. Thus, it is a considerable surprise to realize what a high percentage of new products and concepts are actually introduced by individual entrepreneurs, not by big business.

This is true for many reasons, most of which I've already covered in other contexts. Big business is by nature not an entity that actively seeks or embraces change, and the acceptance of change is essential to innovation. Action (discussed as hunger previously) is certainly present in big business, but what type of action or hunger is there: hunger for developing new concepts (and, hence, new structures) or hunger for the status quo? The answer is obvious. While larger companies may have the fiscal and personnel resources theoretically to effect change, they also carry the ballast of drones and tradition. Driven individuals have neither and are that much more prone to innovation.

While I am not aware of any statistics on what percentage of innovation is generated by newcomers as compared to incumbents, the following thumbnail sketches of just three industries provide a sufficiently impressive example.

1. Transportation. The automobile was not launched by the makers of horse-drawn carriages, nor the airplane by the makers of trains or cars. It was Henry Ford and his ilk who introduced the automotive age, and not even he, but men like the Wright Brothers and later Juan Trippe of Pan Am, who launched us into the skies.

But you could argue that those are the innovations of a former age. What of more recent innovations in transportation?

Well, to start, there have been few significant advances in transportation technology over the past twenty years. The car I drive today is much the same as the one I received on graduation from college back in the sixties. The train I ride between New York and Washington remains very similar to the earliest of diesels. The airplane has hardly changed since the introduction of the jet.

But of course there have been some improvements. But many of the major innovations in transportation technology—from the computer components that make car engines run more efficiently, to the catalytic converters that let them run more cleanly, to the electric vehicle industry that may soon become a major force— were developed by small companies and then sold to the automotive behemoths. New concepts—as distinct from improvements on existing technology—come more often from individuals than from large companies.

Moreover, when it comes to the use of cars or airplanes, the contributions of individuals are even more telling. The largest fleet of planes in America is owned by Federal Express, which was started by the redoubtable Fred Smith. The largest fleets of cars belong to Hertz and Avis, started by Walter L. Jacobs and Warren E. Avis, respectively. Indeed, *every* car rental company was started by one or a group of individuals; not a single one was started by an existing car manufacturer (although for a while the car makers each owned large rental companies).

Admittedly, the largest railroad concern, Amtrak, is a huge public company, heavily publicly subsidized, and by no means entrepreneurial. Then again, it has remained in or near bankruptcy for much of its existence!

2. Food. It is almost a cliché that foods with unique, sharp, or ethnic flavors are launched by small companies, whereas large firms introduce bland food, or copies of whatever other companies already have on the market. Thus:

- The $215 million herbal tea market was launched by Mo Siegel and John Hay of Celestial Seasonings.

- The first major line of premium ice cream, Häagen-Dazs, was started by Reuben Mattus.

- Stouffer's, which revolutionized frozen prepared meals, was founded by Abraham and Mahala Stouffer.

- The most rapidly growing fast-food chain, Boston Market, was created by three entrepreneurs: Steven Kollow, Arthur Cores, and George Naddaff.

- And the first isotonic drink, Gatorade, was introduced by Robert Cade.

Obviously, the food industry encompasses such a wide category of products that large companies, too, have introduced new categories of products. For example, the sugar substitute Equal was created and launched by G. D. Searle & Company (although its predecessor, Sweet'n Low, was the brainchild of an individual entrepreneur, Marvin Eisenstadt). However, even a cursory listing of the contribution of private entrepreneurs, as provided above, suggests how pervasive is their influence.

3. Communications. Arguably the most exciting innovation in how we communicate (and how we shall communicate in the future) is the Internet. It was certainly not the telephone companies, nor the computer giants, nor the huge service supplier like EDS or Microsoft, nor the magazine companies, nor the television networks, who established the Internet. Indeed, as everyone knows, this is the extraordinary achievement of countless individuals, not even the work of any one group of entrepreneurs. It just happened, a new sort of individual, entrepreneurial anarchy that fell together into an unordered but immensely usable whole. (Some might argue that it would be fairer to say that the Internet emerged out of the old ARPANET, funded by the Defense Department and the National Science Foundation. But they did not invent it, even though some of their workers may first have exploited that opportunity to speed up the transfer of information throughout the scientific world. The fact is, it was individuals at universities all over the world who gradually evolved the 'Net—extraordinarily high-achieving individuals at that!)

It was not IBM that launched the software revolution. Indeed, even when individuals such as Bill Gates and Paul Allen of Microsoft actually worked for a large corporation, their employers thought so little of their innovations that they literally ''let them get away'' with the operating system that enabled them to form Microsoft. Moreover, it was Scott Cook of Intuit, Raymond Noorda of Novell, and Mitchell Kapor of Lotus and their ilk who built their sets of software and from them founded their gigantic firms. Moreover, once they did, it was not they who innovated the ubiquitous computer games that have become the pastime preference for 40 million kids. Instead, it was Nolan Bushnell, the creator of Pong, who originally created this rather dubious but undoubtedly successful innovation.

The largest purveyor of cellular telephones in the country was not founded by any of the ''baby bells,'' but by Craig McCaw, an individual. The largest seller of movies is Blockbuster, founded not by MGM or MCA, but by Wayne Huisenga, an individual entrepreneur (who, incidentally, also built the largest toxic chemical disposal firm in the world). And the founder of the modem industry, now generating $1.6 billion in revenues, was not Western Union, but Dennis Hayes, an individual.

Standing in apparent contradiction to the view that most truly new products (as distinct from the refinements of old ones) are created by individuals is the oft-repeated statistic that most new companies fail. A 90 percent failure rate is often cited. On more careful examination, however, this statistic proves to be misleading for two reasons. The first is that this statistic does not refer to "failures" at all, but to companies going out of business. But, obviously, going out of business is in no way equivalent to failure. For example, a company may cease to exist because it acquires another and chooses, for instance for tax purposes, to continue to operate under the acquired company's umbrella. Moreover, frequently companies are established for temporary purposes, for example to develop an office building. They are then disbanded as soon as the project is completed and sold. They ceased to exist because they *succeeded*, not because they failed.

The second reason the statistics are misleading is that there are two separate circumstances when companies actually fail. One is at the very start of the venture. Perhaps they can't raise the money they need or their product or service proves to be unwanted or inoperative, or the founding management is found to be inadequate to the task. These companies do not so much fail as fail to get started. Thus, to lump them together with corporate failures is as meaningless as suggesting that taking a course and failing it is the same as auditing the first lecture and then not taking the course.

The second period of failure, and I believe it is by far the largest instance of entrepreneurial failure, is when the founding entrepreneur has experienced initial start-up success and is now required to convert that into an ongoing business. Phase B, that transition phase between start-up (Phase A) and a mature, largely self-sustaining business (Phase C), is the most troublesome time for most new businesses, and for most founding entrepreneurs, because the very strengths that gave them success in Phase A may prove to be weaknesses in Phase C. As a result, it often takes exceptional individuals of extraordinary caliber to make the changes in their organization and in themselves that are required to achieve this transition. Alternatively, those achievers must have the extraordinary wisdom to abrogate their leadership role voluntarily and turn over the task of transitioning the firm from Phase A to Phase C to lower-achieving, better-trained management professionals, in other words, to experienced facilitators.

PHASE B: THE MANAGEMENT OF RAPIDLY GROWING COMPANIES

The very assets that give the business founder *initial* success may become liabilities that destroy *ongoing* success.

Founding entrepreneurs tend to be highly independent, self-reliant, intuitive, stubbornly opinionated, charismatic, "family"-building patriarchs or matriarchs. Contrary to popular opinion, they are usually surprisingly risk averse, as Stevenson, Roberts, and Grousbeck point out; "It is clear that many entrepreneurs bear risk grudgingly and only after they have made valiant attempts to get the capital sources and resources providers to bear the risk." Indeed, entrepreneurs generally, and perhaps exceptional individuals particularly (for they are prone to "want to get their own way"), usually risk starting a new business only because they just cannot stand being "controlled" by working for someone else. Beyond that, they view being "at risk" as another form of being "controlled," which they cannot abide.

In contrast, CEOs of ongoing businesses tend to be cooperative, team-playing, analytic, open-minded, "faceless" administrators. They are usually quite willing to accept calculated risks. Since it is not their own money they are risking, they can afford to be dispassionate.

In almost every respect, the start-up entrepreneur plays a different role and must exercise different skills than the leader of a mature business. To be more specific, I have identified eight categories in which these changes are most clearly observable, namely:

1. Conceptual Innovation: At the start of a business, the entrepreneur must generate a viable concept. He or she must generate or acquire the idea, *and believe in it.* Later, when the firm is running under its own motivation, the founder may still be the innovator, but the only thing the founder *must* do is to permit innovation—to keep alive the flame. As Collins and Lazier explain in their 1995 book *Managing the Small to Mid-Sized Company,* "In the early phases . . . a company's vision comes directly from its early leaders. . . . To remain healthy . . . the vision must become *shared as a community* and become *identified primarily with the organization* rather than with certain individuals." They conclude quite correctly, "The vision must actually transcend the founders."

2. Driving Force: At the start, if the founder is not the motive force to get things going, the business will never start. But the CEO of the going concern needs to do no more than set the goals for others to achieve. Founding exceptional individuals who stay in the CEO spot may drive forward the organization, but if they are not careful, they may drive it crazy.

3. Motivation: No doubt, when Kentucky Fried Chicken was founded, Colonel Sanders was its charismatic, motivating leader. But today he is no longer alive. Only his image remains as KFC's figurehead. Similarly, Sam Walton is no longer around to jump onto a desk and lead a cheer. Does that mean that the companies they founded will no longer be able to motivate their employees? Obviously, it need not mean that, although if those start-up managers had not planned for their replaceability, it could have that unfortunate effect. The fact is, as Collins and Lazier and others have pointed out, and as I have emphasized earlier, "people will tend to be self-motivated when doing work they believe in" and when they are able to measure the quality of their own performance. The Phase C business leader must establish a positive vision and the self-measurability that will institutionalize motivation—and thus nurture the exceptional individuals' organization needs.

4. Quality Control: At the start of any new business, the quality of its goals or services *is* what the founder designates. The founder "sees all" and will not brook quality below a set standard. Later, however, no individual can assess everything that is happening. Thus, a formal quality-control organization becomes essential to maintaining quality.

5. Raising Funds: Every new business needs money (as discussed in more detail below). At its inception, typically those funds come either from the founder personally or from private sources based on the founder's reputation and business concept. Eventually, however, such private sources no longer suffice. Then more formal bank loans or public stock offerings become necessary. The reputation of the founder has to be replaced by the reputation of firm with the founder's role changing from money *raiser* to money *controller*.

6. Decision Making: Initially, of necessity and of choice, the founder makes all the decisions as I have discussed above. Later, the wise founder does no more than lead the company's teams to make the right decisions.

7. Hiring and Firing: Naturally, the first co-workers to be hired by a start-up organization have to be hired by the founder— and similarly fired if they don't work out. But soon this function (at least for the more junior employees) has to be delegated "down the ladder." Then the founding entrepreneur merely serves as the role model for the type of employee to be hired.

8. Problems: Initially, the problems faced by a new organization are largely unexpected. Since no one has run a business quite like this, no one can predict all the things that are going to go wrong. Thus, it is in the "job description" of any founding entrepreneur that he or she has to solve unexpected problems. But once the business is mature, this changes; then most problems (although rarely all of them) ought to be foreseeable. Thus, the primary job of the CEO becomes avoiding these difficulties.

To summarize, exceptional individuals often succeed gloriously in founding new enterprises. Indeed, most new enterprises are founded by individuals, not by old enterprises. However, the task of converting those start-ups into ongoing nonentrepreneurial businesses requires a wholly different set of skills and even values. Thus, only the rarest of overachievers is fully suited to both the role of Phase A innovator and Phase C manager. Moreover, the ranks of the few who *could* play both parts are further thinned by the many entrepreneurs who simply don't *want* to do so. Thus, it is indeed a rare strain of exceptional individuals, themselves a rare breed, who are Phase B specialists.

Yet the fact that achievers are generally at their best either in Phase A or in Phase C—but not in both—does not in any way diminish my overall thesis, namely, that it is the exceptional individuals who: create successful new businesses; energize successful established businesses; and, as a small class of specialists, effect the transition of one to the other. In any of these instances, it remains true that it is the ability and the hunger of exceptional individuals that leads to the creation and continuation of dynamic and successful businesses.

12

THE EXCEPTIONAL
INDIVIDUAL OF THE FUTURE

If future psychologists or medical scientists succeed in uncovering the keys to the mysteries of the human psyche, then all the motivational and psychological shortcomings in the human animal may someday be erased. However, the greatest leap forward will not come in erasing the defects in the human character, but in allowing all men and women to achieve the full potential of their minds with the aid of new technologies, communication systems, and information sources. These, in turn, will allow future achievers to market more effectively in ways that are today only suggested. How we identify customers and potential customers, in both "targeted" and "mass" approaches, will be specialized to an astonishing degree. And since everyone will have access to these tools, the exceptional individual may one day be the norm.

NEW COMMUNICATION ENHANCES THE POWER OF THE INDIVIDUAL AND THE EXCEPTIONAL INDIVIDUAL

The advances we are making in our ability to communicate with each other are astonishing. Our language ability, far more than our opposable thumbs, has been at the heart of humans' ability to win out in the fight for dominance among all living creatures. The ant, perhaps our closest rival and about our equal in total worldwide bio-weight, has also reached its position of ubiquity and success by a highly advanced communication system, although not nearly as advanced as ours. (Just imagine the power of the indescribably huge hordes of ants if they could talk to each other!)

Thus, the fact that we are living in an age when communication is suddenly leaping forward at speeds and in ways never before imaginable has become the defining circumstance of all aspects of our lives, and certainly of our business lives. We are moving not only into a "knowledge society," as Drucker and many others have written, but into a communication society. Just consider that, within only a few decades, in the sophisticated industrialized nations, there will no longer be "groups" of purchasers, voters, or students. All marketing, politics, and education will be "one on one." And just consider the extra influence and ability to move the world this new approach will provide to the overachiever.

Even today, virtually everything is known about each of us. However, this knowledge is barely used. But soon, with the advent of ubiquitous computerization and interactive communications, all that information will be combined and made available to anyone who wants to buy it. Then consumers will soon be tracked, recognized, and understood *individually*.

High achievers in corporations selling us goods, working for politicians angling for our votes, or in government or private agencies seeking to keep track of us will be able to obtain almost complete information about each of us. Even the illusion of privacy will disappear.

Thus, those people with a penchant for moving things

forward will be able to alter virtually every aspect of our lives, from education to entertainment, from the way we talk to each other to the way we *know* each other, from how we travel to where we travel, in basic ways. Thus, the impact of those people who take the lead in providing us with what we want, the overachievers in our society, will increase exponentially.

One aspect of our lives in particular, namely the way we spend our money, will be dramatically altered. Up to now, even the most dedicated marketing achievers were limited in their impact upon the rest of us because they were forced to consider consumers as if they were large, homogeneous groups: senior citizens, teens, children; baby boomers, yuppies, various "ethnics"; men, women; rich, middle class, poor; urban or rural. Thus, all marketing has been *mass* marketing.

And the impact of such marketing could only be gauged very approximately, since the effect of any single marketing initiative upon a mass of consumers is, at best, barely perceptible. In the future, however, our finances, what we eat, where we shop, our hobbies, our pets, our cars, even our health, will be an open book to marketers. For example, determined achievers in pharmaceutical companies will know when a young couple stops using birth control and, by monitoring the wife's feminine hygiene purchases, when she starts missing her period. They will be able to send them congratulations—and offers for baby products—not long after the woman finds out for herself the happy news that she is pregnant.

Naturally, having this much knowledge about almost all consumers will have a dramatic impact on the marketing industry. For one thing, the effectiveness of advertising in building sales will be instantly visible and precisely measurable. There will be no generalities to hide behind. The difference between advertising that works, that *achieves* its results, and advertising that does not work will be obvious. Thus, the way advertising is written and, importantly, how it is delivered, and, also importantly, by whom, will change fundamentally. The high achievers who know how to write and deliver advertising that really does the job will prosper; the "suits" will fail. And our $150 billion marketing industry will be altered beyond recognition.

Because of this new understanding of each of us as individuals, and the resultant revolution on how we are reached with advertising messages, our whole entertainment industry will also be changed. And, as the string unwinds farther, that will affect everything from education to real estate. Over the next ten years, very little that deals with large numbers of consumers will remain the way it is today.

Taking the lead in the commercialization of these trends will be a number of individuals. This has always been so when the circumstances have been ripe for rapid change. But it will be even more true in the future, for, if we can be reached as individuals rather than as members of a group, that is if our individuality becomes a matter of greater importance to marketers than it is today, then our ability to reach out will increase commensurately. The power of all individuals, both as consumers of information (and things) and as the communicators of information and the purveyors of things, will greatly increase. And, of course, the power of those individuals who really make things happen will increase more rapidly still.

Most of our information about what to buy, whom to vote for, how to live, is derived from uniform messages delivered to large masses of us. Whether those messages come from television, magazines, newspapers, or various forms of sales promotion, they all force our purchasing patterns and options—and our daily information intake—into a uniform pattern. But it is my contention that this pattern is formed and offered to us by a surprisingly small number, representing a tiny percentage, of the people involved in administering the effort.

The advent of new technology in every field from bioengineering to steel manufacture is daily increasing the product options we have available. Thus, from drugs to foods, from cars to clothing, our choices are constantly expanding. Bookstores have experimented with customized books where buyers can compile their own content from a vast selection of options. "Bespoke" tailoring, which died out when our grandfathers switched to off-the-rack suits, is making a computer-assisted comeback. Their own personal hair color recipe keeps women returning to beauty salons. Our local hardware stores are the only places in the world that know what color paint we used two years ago to decorate our living rooms. And, as our choices expand, so will the ability of those relatively few people who catalyze their creation to influence us all.

Beyond that, our jobs are becoming more individualized through flex time, working at home, and a strong trend toward increased specialization. Thus, there will be more opportunities for people with the urge to get things done to move into influential positions.

Similarly, advertising messages and programs that carry advertising are becoming individualized both in content and in delivery. Thus, while marketing will remain "the art and science of selling to more people than you can talk to personally," it will change in fundamental ways. Paul Allen, co-founder of Microsoft, defines this change as "the marriage of video technology, computer technology, and networking" and calls it "the incredible wave that's coming." That wave will mean that video technology will soon allow marketers to reach us individually; computer technology will enable them to describe and define us individually. The long arm of the marketer will become far more powerful than we have ever before imagined. And thus the power, and importance, of those men and women who dominate the action within the companies that market will become even more impressive.

Such individualization will mean that programming will be specifically tailored to each of us; it will mean, too, that any interested party will be able to know a great deal about our personal tastes, our purchasing habits, and our behavior patterns. From purchasing to voting, from vocations to vacations, much of what we do and who we are as individuals will be an open book to anyone interested in reading it. Thus, not only will we be able to define people as consumers by analyzing any number of their consumption patterns and behaviors, but we shall also be able to isolate and approach individually those people who achieve more than others. The illusive "influencers" in our society, the Tryers of New Things, the people whose new car causes their whole block to change their automotive buying habits, will become visible. Both as influencers of consumption and as creators of production, the exceptional individuals will become even more central to our lives.

Consider just three of the major techniques that people of achievement will have available to impact every one of us:

1. Tailored Programming: Interactive television will eventually allow us to chose from a huge variety of programming. To add even more to that variety, we shall be able to use interactivity to assemble our own shows from a vast selection of available "pieces" of programming.

What we choose to watch, and what we include in the "packages of entertainment" we assemble for ourselves, will define our interests, enthusiasms, and dislikes. It used to be said that people "are what they read." Because they had a wide choice of books, which ones they read said much about them. It will soon be more true that "we are what we watch."

Even more important than the fact that we watch different shows is that the shows' distributors will know what we watch and will be able to record what actions we take as a result of watching. If we don't buy products advertised on a given show, its owners will not beam it to us even if we happen to enjoy it—unless, of course, we are prepared to pay for it. After all, someone has to pay for the show, either we or the advertisers. And why should the advertiser pay for me individually to see the show if I do not buy the advertised product? There is no reason at all. Once the advertiser knows that I am unresponsive to the products advertised, I will no longer be beamed the advertising—or the show.

2. Knowing Individual Tastes: As more and more forms of "moving images" become available (ranging from mail-order sales of specialized videos to computer communication via visually sophisticated offerings on the Internet), high-achieving marketers and other communicators will be able to track exactly what we select from the virtually limitless variety available. As a result, they will know what interests us, what we think about and believe in, perhaps even what we dream. These data, compiled to present detailed profiles of each of us, will be available for purchase by any interested party.

3. Tracking Purchases: What we buy in large measure describes how we live and what interests us. And what we buy is becoming almost totally known by savvy marketers in at least three ways:

a. The exploding category of direct purchasing is generating detailed data about each of us. What we buy through the mail or by phone becomes part of the permanent record of our purchase patterns.

b. Virtually all food and drug products now carry a "universal code." Thus, retailers know every product each of us buys in their stores if we identify ourselves by paying by check or credit card. By tracking our purchases over time, they can obtain a surprisingly complete picture of our market basket and the living habits and conditions it implies. For example, a retailer can determine by looking at our purchases of cat food if a cat arrived or left the family. To date, these purchase patterns, while collected by many individual retail chains, have not been tied together. However, Citicorp made a serious attempt to do so in the late 1980s. They aborted the attempt because of management problems and a corporate profit squeeze. But they ran it long enough to show that the approach is practical and will become economically viable. There seems little doubt that before long someone will institute a program like the one Citicorp abandoned.

c. There are many organizations that track other information about us. For example, individual companies already know: from car registration lists, what cars we drive, and on what schedule we replace them; from high school and university records, our educational levels; from public records, our marital status; from travel agencies, airlines, and hotels, where we travel; and from a wide variety of sources, our financial standing and credit-worthiness, our employment history, our hobbies, our health, our family lives, and what motivates us.

So far, these three sets of knowledge have not been combined into an overall profile of each of us. There has been insufficient economic incentive to know us individually because we could not be reached individually. However, as the ability to reach us expands, so will the value of our individual profiles. And as computer capacity increases exponentially, it will become far less expensive to "hook together" all the sources of information about us to generate an ever more detailed description of each of us. Before long, each of us will be known individually to all marketers, communicators, politicians, and anyone else who wants to know. These institutions will know us, one by one, in extraordinary detail, our name, address, income, education, faith, health, interests, purchasing patterns, and motivators. Thus the impact upon each of us by those individuals who create the action in our suppliers, that is, those achievers who will become the givers of our choices, will become awesome.

INFORMATION SOURCES WILL GROW EXPLOSIVELY

One of the little-thought-about facts of our daily lives is that most of our daily information comes via advertising-supported media. Nearly all the television we see, the radio we hear, and the newspapers and magazines we read are financed in major part by advertising. Most of our understanding of current events, political movements, fashion trends, and even cultural developments stems from these media. Thus, it is no exaggeration to say that advertisers finance the large majority of the institutions that furnish us with information.

Regarding more basic or "in-depth" information (beyond the scope of the popular media), the hard fact is that less than 5 percent of the population reads eight books or more a year, and only a small percentage of the adult, post-college population participates in any formal learning program outside the workplace. Thus, apart from advertiser-supported information, the only other significant source of our ongoing education is commercially supported, on-the-job training (including work-related seminars and training courses). These commercially sponsored educational efforts are of vast scope and account for most of the training and education we need for our working lives.

Since the information-purveying media are *mass* advertiser supported, they will change dramatically over time as they become *individual* advertiser supported. Moreover, significant parts of on-the-job training are today "mass" developed with standard teaching curricula and textbooks. These, too, will have to become "individualized." And, of course, part of that individualization will be the separate and careful fostering, nurturing, and training of the individuals with a potential for achievement, so as to turn the potential into its actuality.

Both in the media and, to a lesser extent, in all types of teaching, individual programming will slowly replace mass programming. Those of us who are not interested in weather, cops and robbers, and women's issues—or, even if interested, do not respond well to advertising messages beamed into those environments—will rarely be exposed to such programming. Thus, our access to information in which we have expressed no particular interest in the past will be curtailed. We shall tend to become ever more knowledgeable about an ever-decreasing group of interests.

Similarly, on the job, we shall be taught to an ever greater extent those things we need to know in order to do our specific jobs better. Why should a company pay to provide employees with knowledge they do not immediately need and that contributes nothing to their handling of their current jobs? Even if such broader knowledge were known to be of value later in employees' careers, employers, having no assurance that such value would accrue to them given the ever-increasing mobility of employees, would hardly expend heavy funds on such education. Rather, on-the-job training will tend to add more and more "depth" to our current jobs—and thus tend strongly to make us ever more specialized. For most people, both via media and on the job, the availability of information will be truncated. There will be a rising tendency for such average people to be exposed only to categories of information with which they are already familiar and comfortable. In contrast, exceptional individuals, who demonstrate by their actions that they are broadly interested and responsive to new ideas, new products, new education, will have the benefit of being exposed to a vast wealth of these inputs. High achievers will thus be "hot-housed" to become ever more effective at getting things done.

MARKETING WILL EMPOWER OVERACHIEVERS

With the aforementioned changes in technology, the institutions of marketing will change drastically over the next few years. Already, it is think tanks, staffed by scientists and computer experts, not the leading advertising, promotion, and media-buying agencies or the traditional communications companies, who are in the vanguard of determining what sort of goods and services the "information highway" of the future will need. Huge advertising agencies, now "factories of mass communication" living off their ability to write clever ads and maintain personal relationships with their clients, will be transmogrified into (or replaced by) software-driven organizations capable of targeting consumers with specific purchase incentives. The important and valuable skills for marketing practitioners of the future will be desktop publishing, desktop video, facility with the Internet, effectiveness in all forms of computer communication, and the ability to understand the new world of one-on-one selling. Cleverness and personal contacts will count for little compared to selling effectiveness, that is, the real achievement rather than merely the appearance of it. Already among certain computer-centered individuals, "real life" meetings are becoming so rare that they are specifically designated as "IRL" (in real life) meetings.

The reason personal contact and IRL meetings will become less important is that the effectiveness of agencies' services will be measurable by unarguable results. An advertising campaign that does not pay for itself in terms of new business will be discontinued promptly; and, after a few such misfires, so will the agency that prepared it—regardless of the degree of personal contact between agency and company executives.

In general, two forms of advertising will exist in the future: "Directed" advertising, akin to today's advertising but targeted individually and therefore with far greater impact per viewer than at present; and "Requested" advertising, which consumers will seek out as they now "request" QVC and infomercials.

Directed advertising, messages directed at a specific audience, involves two considerations:

1. In order to select audiences known to be interested and responsive, and then to influence them to buy, advertisers will record exactly which goods and services individuals purchase

as a result of being exposed to which messages. Once this is known, every message will be tailored precisely to an individual viewer's actual and potential needs, wants, and known motivators (such as promotions, advertising messages, or price reductions). These individually crafted messages will then be beamed separately to each individual. All these data are or will be purchasable.

2. Marketers may select the audience for their marketing message by selling them something connected to that message. For example, selling valuable beer mugs at a large discount is obviously one way of attracting a large number of beer drinkers. At a more sophisticated level, by offering books on specific subjects, marketers will be able to attract audiences very precisely attuned to their own products.
   In each such case, these peripheral wares will be sold at deep discounts because their buyers are the natural marketing targets for the marketers' product and thus have a greater dollar value to the marketer than the cost of the discount.

Requested advertising will reach fewer people, but of course they will be prime prospects: They, quite literally, "asked for it." This applies today to the television shopping networks to which consumers turn knowing that they will be viewing selling messages exclusively. However, in the future, in order to induce more such "requests," advertisers will seek to make their messages more interesting by adding noncommercial programming into the mix. Eventually, therefore, some requested advertising will actually be requested for the "wrong" reasons, i.e., for the quality of its programming. Thus, requested advertising will merge with directed advertising; there will not always be a clear-cut delineation. What will be clear-cut is the cost effectiveness of every message to each consumer: Only messages that make money for their advertiser will survive. Thus, the people who are effective in creating the right messages (and the right goods or services about which to send the messages) will not only survive, but gain ever more influence. Exceptional individuals will become ever more central to the success of business.

13

THE FULL INFLUENCE OF THE EXCEPTIONAL INDIVIDUAL

Despite flabbergasting human progress, the abilities of the exceptional individual as discussed in this book remain beyond the reach of artificial development. It cannot yet be injected like a truth serum, or taught in business schools, or supplied via correspondence courses. Personal excellence cannot even be neatly summarized as if it were the formula for a new drug. Although some people seem to attain personal excellence from a near-miraculous drive coupled with the shrewd intelligence and other traits I have defined, the exact formula for their success cannot be duplicated because it resides within the individual. However, as I have tried to show, such excellence can be fostered and maximized. And it must be thus supported, for it not only lies at the root and heart of all business success but, far more, it actually constitutes and directs the very essence of human evolutionary success.

Henry David Thoreau, the patron saint of today's back-to-nature advocates, retired to Walden Pond "to live deliberately, to front only the essential facts of life, and see if I could not learn what it had to teach." His goal was never to become a hermit or some eccentric recluse. It was, in fact, a far more noble—and nobly human—goal, the ultimate achiever's objective: "to live deep and suck out the marrow of life."

Humans have risen from the "primeval ooze" and prospered through a long series of evolutionary challenges. From our continuing evolution will someday rise new and greater human creatures than we can even dream of. It is my article of faith to believe that it is inevitable that our current evolutionary pinnacle will be topped, and topped again. The drive to achievement is self-perpetuating, the need for improvement nonending in a certain type of human. And yet imperfection, too, is a part of our human condition. Thus, it is our very human weaknesses that are driving the process of our improvement. I find it useful, exciting, and wonderfully energizing to allow myself to think of human evolution as driven by the achievements of those exceptional individuals who dedicate themselves to achievement—and thus aspire to personal excellence. We can all be part of it, I conclude with smug and wonderful confidence. Even if we are only the facilitators of achievement, we need not be totally left out.

Similarly, I dare to assume that, at this moment, we are living within the start-up of a new evolutionary advance of lasting value. If so, then you and I exist in an incredibly exciting moment, almost (but not quite) beyond the grasp of our imagination, but not at all beyond our collective ability to implement, led, as always, by some *individuals'* ability to show the "collective" the way.

For surely it is the exceptional individuals in our society, by my definition those rare individuals who move matters forward, who are the actual implementors of this evolutionary change we are experiencing. Obviously, my intuitive, self-centered evaluation of the importance of personal excellence is not yet buttressed by hard science. But as a platform upon which to build the world of the future, I believe that it is the exceptional individuals among us—and not of any techniques, theories, or preordained set of rules, laws, or theorems—that is fundamental. I have found no other platform of comparable utility.

After all, it is achievement that makes life worth living, not only because of material rewards, although those are important, but primarily because achievement nurtures the human spirit. Achievement provides a deep, almost primitive satisfaction. Great achievement provides great enjoyment and great meaning and helps to fulfill life. Personal excellence provides the instinctive thrill of pulling humanity one step farther away from the ooze from which we rose, and one step farther into the future. In *Walden*, Henry Thoreau wrote:

> *I know of no more encouraging fact, than the unquestionable ability of man to elevate his life by a conscious endeavor. It is something to be able to paint a particular picture, or to carve a statue, and so to make a few objects beautiful; but it is far more glorious to carve and paint the very atmosphere and medium through which we look, which morally we can do. To affect the quality of the day, that is the highest of arts. Every man is tasked to make his life, even in its details, worthy of the contemplation of his most elevated and critical hour.*

If you seek to achieve such personal excellence, then sacrifice becomes worthwhile, and even immense effort is no sacrifice at all, but a kind of joyful giving. Like the humanitarian prayer from the Unitarian Church, achievement at the highest level is accomplished "so that we may justify our existence in time; and render glory to that which is eternal." Striving for personal excellence, the credo of every exceptional individual I have ever met, has not the goal of taking material things from life, but of contributing those things to life—and thus of building upon and helping to secure the glory of human progress.

And this progress demands an economic component. We cannot move forward socially without a strong economic state. This is a fact that even the most ardent ideologist must acknowledge. And business plays a vital role. Business creates wealth. Compare countries in today's world and prove the obvious to yourself. Where rich economies exist, a solid infrastructure of wealthy business supports them. Where there are poor economies, workers are poor because they are not supported by wealthy businesses. Of course without wealthy businesses, the layer of the "rich" is exceedingly thin (limited, for the most part, to the rulers, the aristocracy, and warlords who exploit everyone else).

Since 1969, all levels of American society did, in fact, become wealthier, although the gap between rich and poor widened. Millions of new businesses opened. Over short economic periods, this may not be true since economic trends do not follow smooth patterns. But in the long run, as the economic welfare of a country improves, the rich get richer and the poor get richer, too. And, billowing clouds of myths to the contrary notwithstanding, the gap between rich and poor has been narrowing for hundreds of years. To maintain this steady progress will be one of the great challenges—and, I am sure, one of the great achievements—of those exceptional individuals who, through their own personal excellence, are capable of "getting things done."

As companies restructure and shed jobs at alarming rates of speed, people must be retrained for new ones, sometimes several times in one lifetime. One challenge for our exceptional individuals is to solve this huge societal problem of educating and employing all people, facilitators and drones as well as the achievers themselves, and thus to make the lives of all men and women vibrant, secure, and productive.

A related challenge for our society is to build a new layer of businesses in our inner cities. To lift up whole populations by their bootstraps will certainly call for more exceptional individuals. More importantly, however, within our growing communications society, it will become obvious (and no longer as it is today politically incorrect to mention) that our underprivileged populations are just that: less educated, less healthy, less productive, less capable of being productive not because they are inferior, but because they have had withheld from them the opportunity both of cultural heritage and of contemporary education.

Once we are willing to admit that, in America at least, our primary problem lies not in health or education or drugs, but in a minority population that has inadequate education and suffers from a lack of historical "privilege," we shall be well on the way to allowing the high achievers in our nation to implement a solution. For while the genesis of the problem is both perfectly obvious and most regrettable, the regrets are irrelevant to solving it, whereas identifying it is key to finding its solution. Soon, with ever more communication efficiency, we shall be able to define the problem, and state the truth about it, without being accused of racism or bias.

ADAM SMITH AT THE MILLENNIUM

In the very new and different world of the twenty-first century, where wealth will be based on knowledge, information, and communication, it will remain just as true as in the past, where wealth was created by manufacturing prowess, that no system will drive business. Only exceptional individuals who embody personal excellence and meet all types of challenges, dealing with them pragmatically and often creatively, but never by rote or reflex, can provide that motive force.

True, the past ten years have been traumatic for many, a decade in which greed and gluttony triumphed in some quarters, and in which significant changes in the composition of the workforce occurred. As various individuals made and lost huge fortunes, some via questionable business practices and insider dealings, many good people were thrown out of work through no particular fault of their own because our largest companies were hiring or retiring hundreds of thousands of employees.

Simultaneously, the number of freelance people working temporary jobs has tripled in the past ten years. Clearly, new types of jobs are being created by new types of companies. Such new ideas and successful new enterprises are always created and always nurtured by the exceptional individuals.

We are still seeing the fallout from years of short-sighted management in big business, from years of forgetting that it is people, not systems, that drive businesses to success. As a result, between 1985 and 1995, the percentage of people employed full time by Fortune 500 companies dropped from more than 20 percent to only about 10 percent of the American workforce. However, small companies understood far better the importance of exceptional individuals. While big companies eliminated about 3.7 million positions during the past ten years, small companies created some 20 million jobs.

At this moment, many large corporations are still frantically "restructuring" or reengineering. Where their purpose is to let their exceptional individuals work more effectively, their efforts may succeed; where such firms are following a consultant-recommended technique and failing to give full honor, credence, and reward to the people implementing it, they will probably fail.

THE NECESSITY OF THE EXCEPTIONAL INDIVIDUAL

Which brings us back to the men and women who create the motive power in business, the people who aspire to achievement, and who measure their own personal "excellence" by looking at results, not at hopes, promises, or excuses. The development, training, and motivation of such business leaders and employees is more than important today: it is vital. The men and women who move our businesses forward are ushering in an entirely new age. While no one views them, as they did the monarchs of the past, as divinely anointed, the fact remains that these exceptional individuals possess the power. They hold our future within their implementation capacity. Thus, we are relying on them not only to move the world forward, but to do so quickly, wisely, and judiciously.

The men or women who will lead the business of the next century will necessarily have wholly different skills than today's exceptional individuals, and quite possibly the business objectives themselves will change dramatically. But the magical motive force, the hunger for achievement, the yearning for personal excellence, will remain. Moreover, as knowledge and its communication become ever more central to achievement, no company will be able to brook the kind of "attitude" that led an early Lever Brothers graffiti artist to scrawl across the company's organization charts:

Across this tree
From root to crown
Ideas flow up
And vetoes down

Even more in the admittedly only murkily defined future than today, business will not be able to survive if it follows the by-rote rules of some consultant's technique rather than demanding management achievement. It remains true today that the difference between a "growth industry" and one that isn't growing is executive perspective, as Ted Levitt pointed out in his famous essay, "Marketing Myopia." That perspective will become even more essential in the future. In a dynamic world marketplace, with ever more knowledgeable workers, faster and more complete communications, and vast new technologies to tame and exploit, achievement will involve decisions of direction, not just of degree. That is, not only will business be called upon to improve products and services as it has been ever since the start of the industrial revolution, but it will also be required to decide on which direction to pursue. That is a degree of responsibility never before placed upon business. It will require the clear-sighted perspective of men and women who have the self-confidence, dynamism, intelligence, and desire for achievement, that is the hunger, to make these new, tougher, more telling decisions.

Profit is and will necessarily remain the yardstick of business success. The profits made by businesspeople may be used for eleemosynary purposes, but the activity of the business in the first place is to generate those profits. However, if consumers cry for business to support the common good in addition to producing good products or good services, then businesspeople will be well advised to listen carefully to exactly what that cry means—and then respond appropriately. Perhaps, as a result, we may reach for a new standard of business morality. As business finds it prudent to cater to new consumer demands, profits and public service will become ever more entwined. Once again, this will be a matter of reaching a balanced level of achievement. A sense of perspective and the courage to act on it are the hallmarks of exceptional individuals.

Business stretches its arms into every facet of human life. Business influences or perhaps controls education, health, culture, world politics—and ultimately peace. To deal with such disparate and mammoth responsibilities, business achievers must, in addition to the hunger to achieve, also develop the ability, the perspective, to compromise.

Arthur Waley described the triumph of Confucianism as "due in large measure to the fact that it contrived to endow compromise with an emotional glamour." The exceptional individuals of the future will need to recognize compromise as being emotionally glamorous. As businesses downsize, rightsize, diversify, and communicate with each of us one-on-one, new solutions to the problems of society as a whole will be created by individuals within corporations large and small. In implementing these untried solutions, people will need to achieve compromises that accelerate action. "The true gentleman is conciliatory, but not accommodating. Common people are accommodating but not conciliatory," said Confucius the Master. The "true gentlemen" in modern business are the exceptional individuals. They will continue to create the actions necessary to move business forward, and thus to move forward our world.